SUCCESSFUL GARDENING

COLOUR ROUND
THE YEAR

Published by The Reader's Digest Association Limited.

First Edition Copyright © 1991
The Reader's Digest Association Limited,
Berkeley Square House, Berkeley Square, London W1X 6AB

Copyright © 1991
The Reader's Digest Association Far East Limited
Philippines Copyright 1991
The Reader's Digest Association Far East Limited
Reprinted 1992

® READER'S DIGEST
is a registered trademark of
The Reader's Digest Association Inc. of Pleasantville,
New York, USA

Consultant editor: Lizzie Boyd

Typeset by SX Composing Limited in Century Schoolbook

PRINTED IN SPAIN

ISBN 0 276 42041 1

Front cover: Golden day lilies (*Hemerocallis*)
dominate a herbaceous border of pastel shades.

Back cover: Virginia creeper (*Parthenocissus
quinquefolia*) turns brilliant purple and
crimson before leaf-fall.

Opposite: Tall, clear pink tree mallows (*Lavatera olbia* ×
'Hosea') tower above blue *Agapanthus* 'Headbourne
Hybrids' and tiny daisy-flowered *Felicia amelloides*.

Overleaf: The orange-yellow blooms of evergreen *Berberis*
× *stenophylla* 'Etna' glow against a blue-green
background of *Picea pungens glauca*.

PUBLISHED BY THE READER'S DIGEST ASSOCIATION LIMITED
LONDON NEW YORK MONTREAL SYDNEY CAPE TOWN

Originally published in partwork form
by Eaglemoss Publications Limited

SUCCESSFUL GARDENING

COLOUR ROUND
THE YEAR

Colour round the year

In a well-planned garden, colours gently change as the seasons progress from the fresh tints of spring, through summer's highlights to autumn's fiery glow and the subdued tones of winter. The garden picture need never be dull since with forethought and planning, the framework created by trees and shrubs in a range of leaf colours, and by foliage plants in silver, gold and purple can become a fitting background for a variety of colour schemes that echo through the seasons.

One preference may be for pale colours, on their own, complemented by other pastel shades or contrasted with bold primaries. Other choices may centre around vibrant scarlet or mauve, or an exuberant mixture of all the colours of the rainbow.

This book inspires and invites readers to experiment with colour combinations and group plantings to keep the garden alive throughout the twelve months of the year.

CONTENTS

Year-round colour Evergreen foliage provides a perfect backdrop for a palette of colours.

Colour creations

Each of the four seasons has its own particular motif in the garden. The crocus and daffodils of spring give way to roses and lilies in summer; the dahlias and chrysanthemums of autumn are followed by winter jasmine and snowdrops. Between these floral highlights there is an enormous range of other plants that create a vibrant tapestry of colours. With thoughtful planning, it is possible to have a garden in which the seasons are echoed by a progression of colour combinations and associations.

Like the progress of the year, the colour spectrum in the garden follows the sun. Gentle pastel shades of primroses and forget-me-nots mirror the weak spring sun, which warms to the golden hues of crown imperials and the reds and blues of rhododendrons, until it bursts upon the glorious colour of the summer garden. As the sun lowers and the shadows lengthen, the fierce colours of autumn are reflected in harvest-ripe fruit and blazing red and golden foliage. But even when the leaves have fallen, the garden is not dead; the evergreen blanket of hollies and conifers shelters blossoming winter heathers and Christmas roses.

One of the most rewarding garden activities is arranging and grouping plants next to each other. Few enjoy isolated splendour, but their loveliness is enhanced by suitable companions. Rather than dotting plants around in a kaleidoscope of colours, think about planning groups of complementary tones that melt into harmonious pictures, with pastel shades to soften dramatic colour schemes and to create pools of light in sombre corners.

Symbols of spring Daffodils hover above primroses, fritillaries and white ipheions.

BURSTS OF SPRING COLOUR

**Rising temperatures and gentle showers bring on
a rush of flowering bulbs, shrubs and perennials in colourful
partnerships through the spring months.**

As spring advances, more and more colour brightens the garden scene until, in the warmth of late May, it is fully furnished. Flowering shrubs and trees, woodland and border perennials, early bedding plants, fresh young foliage and bulbs and alpines provide rich material for creating a number of colourful pictures.

Spurges, for example, are interesting plants with colourful bracts. Perennial *Euphorbia polychroma* forms a bushy mound about 45cm (1½ft) in all directions, covered with bright yellow bracts. For an effective association, partner it with the vertical lines of Bowles' golden grass (*Milium effusum* 'Aureum') and yellow tulips in front.

Yellow tulips, too, can be used with flame-coloured wallflowers – both planted in blocks at the front of a mixed border. White tulips showing through a blue sea of forget-me-nots form a beautiful contrast in the spring sunshine – or use pink tulips for harmony.

Create a blue and white association with white flowering *Bergenia stracheyi* 'Silberlicht' set against a background of the airy forget-me-not-like sprays of 45cm (1½ft) high Siberian bugloss (*Brunnera macrophylla*). Introduce more blue with clumps of scilla-like Spanish bluebell (*Endymion hispanicus*), whose glossy strap-shaped leaves contrast well with the rather coarser foliage of its companions.

The great white chalices of *Magnolia* × *soulangiana* are stained pinkish purple at their bases, a colour that can be enhanced by an underplanting of lungwort (*Pulmonaria saccha-rata*), whose pink and blue flowers are backed by hairy, silver marked leaves, and the native wood anemone (*Anemone nemorosa*), with white bowl-shaped flowers often flushed pink.

The blue-flowered evergreen *Ceanothus* × 'Delight', which needs the shelter of a warm wall, blooms in late spring. For a pretty combination train the soft pink *Clematis montana* 'Elizabeth' on the wall behind; in front set the white-flowered Mexican orange (*Choisya ternata*) with its sweetly scented star-like flowers that pick up the shape of the clematis.

▼ **Spring bedding** Stout hyacinths, clear coloured and sweetly scented, associate perfectly with Greigii hybrid tulips whose broad, wavy-edged leaves are striped and mottled with purple.

◄ Spring blossom Pink azaleas peep through the immaculate white blossom of a crab apple in this evocative border scene, and a young *Kerria japonica* already weaves its golden flowers above a carpet of blue forget-me-nots and pink saxifrages. In autumn, the crab apple takes centre stage again, with crops of golden-red fruit and handsome tints to the foliage.

▼ Colour contrast Cheerful golden daisies of leopard's bane (*Doronicum plantagineum*), carried some 60cm (2ft) above hairy heart-shaped leaves, provide bold contrast in colour and form to mats of aubrietas in shades of blue, purple, red and pink. Clothing rock gardens, dry walls and sunny banks, aubrietas also make vibrant front edgings for borders and beds.

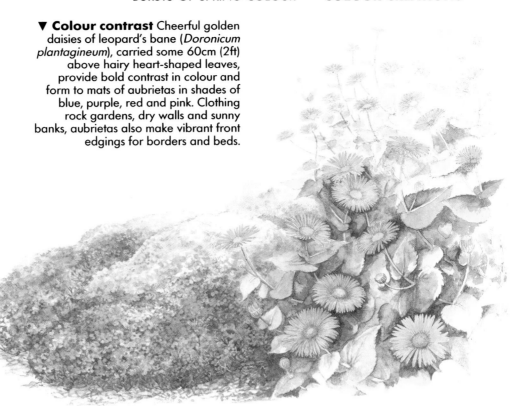

▼ Sea of blue The double-flowered grape hyacinth, *Muscari armeniacum* 'Blue Spike', increases steadily, spreading over the ground beneath deciduous trees and shrubs. The sheet of bright blue is broken here and there with the scarlet goblets of Greigii hybrid tulips which also naturalize well in gentle shade.

▶ Spring showers

Dappled shade over rich moist soil entices the wake robin (*Trillium grandiflorum*) to open its white three-petalled flowers. It blooms in mid and late spring, at the same time as its low-growing companion, the American trout lily (*Erythronium revolutum*), with nodding, lily-like flowers above distinctive mottled leaves.

▼ Majestic splendour

The aristocrat of spring, the crown imperial (*Fritillaria imperialis*) is spectacular in full bloom. Whorls of bell-like flowers, lemon-yellow in the variety 'Lutea', are carried proudly atop tall leafy stems. At its feet are ground-covering *Viola labradorica* 'Purpurea' and the white, yellow-centred blooms of *Tulipa tarda*.

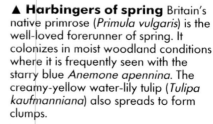

▲ **Harbingers of spring** Britain's native primrose (*Primula vulgaris*) is the well-loved forerunner of spring. It colonizes in moist woodland conditions where it is frequently seen with the starry blue *Anemone apennina*. The creamy-yellow water-lily tulip (*Tulipa kaufmanniana*) also spreads to form clumps.

SUMMER GLORY

**Blazing colours, luxuriant foliage
and heady scents epitomize the long
hazy days of summer.**

After the delights of spring, with its delicate displays of bulbs and other early-flowering plants, mixed and herbaceous borders come into their own. Clumps of perennials fill their allotted spaces and colour is more vibrant. It is the time for roses, mock oranges, peonies, bearded irises, old-fashioned pinks, lilies, annuals and bedding plants.

When planning associations for this season, remember that much of the gardening year is still to come, so space must be left for later-flowering plants. Use their mounds of fresh green foliage, with promise of further colour, as a background or foil.

The choice of plants that flower throughout the summer months is overwhelming, tempting us to cram as many different varieties as possible into borders. Resist this, and aim instead for simple partnerships, using several plants of the same species for large and bold effect. The result will be more interesting and restful than one with numerous varieties in different shapes and colours.

It is quite possible to create a grouping with only one flowering variety, the rest of the 'canvas' consisting of beautiful foliage. Try planting several corms of the hardy *Gladiolus byzantinus*, which has magenta flowers (often

▲ **Early summer** Sweet William (*Dianthus barbatus*) takes over where spring left off. Plant in bold groups at the front of a border and against a backdrop of foliage from shrubs that have finished flowering.

a colour difficult to place), among the low-growing variegated shrub *Euonymous fortunei* 'Silver Queen'. They will increase year after year, and the shrub's silvery-white variegation sets off the one-sided spikes of the gladiolus.

If you can't resist several flowering varieties together, a pretty, cottage garden effect can be obtained by combining three annuals: baby's breath (*Gypsophila elegans*), love-in-a-mist (*Nigella damascena*) and larkspur (*Delphinium ajacis*). Baby's breath grows to about 45-60cm (1½-2ft) tall and has grey-green leaves with masses of small white (sometimes pink) flowers. The blue or white love-in-a-mist is about the same height so plant it beside the baby's breath. Larkspur has blue, pink or white flowers and is best placed behind the others because its stately flower spikes can reach 90cm (3ft) high. The result is a delicate, misty combination of soft pastels.

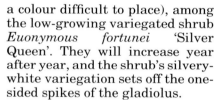

◄ **High summer** This colourful group of low-growing plants will be in bloom for several months. Dominated by a yellow potentilla (*Potentilla fruticosa*) and a pink rock rose (*Helianthemum nummularium*), the blue *Campanula portenschlagiana* and red crane's bill (*Geranium sanguineum*) attempt to exceed their allotted space.

▶ **Study in pink** The perennial border phlox flowers for many summer weeks, revelling in full sun and enjoying the company of cerise-pink mallows (*Lavatera trimestris*) and low-growing *Godetia grandiflora*. A front edging of matching and contrasting petunias completes the composition.

▼ **High summer** Backed by the tea-scented hybrid musk rose 'Buff Beauty', this long-flowering group creates a pool of soft colours. Tall lavender-blue *Campanula lactiflora* 'Pritchard's Variety' complement the white, purple-streaked trumpets of *Lilium regale*, their feet shrouded in an edging of pink *Geranium endressii* and lemon-scented *Thymus* × *citriodorus*.

▲ Shady borders The Himalayan poppy (*Meconopsis betonicifolia*) demands light shade for its magnificent cups of clearest blue whose golden stamens are perfectly echoed in the shade-loving *Lonicera × tellmanniana*. Elegant hostas occupy the foreground displaying arching mounds of golden foliage.

◄ Sun revellers Annual *Zinnia elegans* produces dahlia-like blooms in a richly coloured tapestry, ideal for filling gaps in the herbaceous border. Tall spikes of stately blue delphiniums provide a dramatic background for a planting of sneezeweed (*Helenium autumnale* 'Bressingham Gold') whose golden-bronze flowers, suffused with crimson, persist through summer and into autumn.

▲ **Late summer** Strong reds can be difficult to place in the herbaceous border. Here, a clump of flame-red montbretias (*Crocosmia* 'Lucifer') is successfully partnered with the cerise-pink daisy flowers of the annual *Senecio elegans*, seen on a dramatically purple background of *Berberis thunbergii* 'Rose Glow'. The airy, silvery-blue leaves of *Eucalyptus gunnii* provide welcome contrast in colour and form.

◄ **Flower power** After months of warm sunshine, half-hardy annuals put on a final, late-summer show of colour before they succumb to the first autumn frost. White-eyed, purple *Lobelia erinus* tumble over the edges of this window box, happy companions to the free-flowering but compact little *Nemesia strumosa* whose funnel-shaped flowers come in shades of cream, yellow, blue, orange and crimson, often with spotted throats.

MELLOW AUTUMN TINTS

**Early morning dew and fading light herald
the autumn, but flowers, berries and turning leaves
provide a wealth of colour in the garden.**

With careful planning, early autumn can offer plenty of interest in the garden: late-flowering shrubs and perennials will be in full splendour and, as a bonus, leaves are turning, fruits are ripening, and the first autumn bulbs are emerging.

Herbaceous borders tend to be dominated by the daisy family at this time of year, with heleniums, helianthus, golden rod, rudbeckias, and Michaelmas daisies in bloom. Since most of these have daisy-like flowerheads it pays to introduce some contrast, with perhaps the upright spikes of late-flowering red hot pokers, the large pale pink and white saucer-shaped blooms of Japanese anemones or a clump of *Sedum* 'Autumn Joy'.

In the shrub border, hydrangeas and hardy fuchsias are an important source of colour. Other late-flowering shrubs include pretty *Caryopteris* × *clandonensis* and *Ceratostigma willmottianum*. Both have blue blooms which look most attractive partnered with exotic *Amaryllis belladonna*, a slightly tender, autumn-flowering bulb with enormous, pink trumpet-shaped flowers held 60-75cm (2-2½ft) above ground.

Heather (*Calluna vulgaris*) is another autumn favourite, best grown in a mass on its own. However, varieties developed from this species offer such an enormous range of flower colours (pinks, purples, reds and whites) and foliage colours (green, gold, bronze and silver) that you can create an eye-catching picture using just these heathers.

For accents of hot colour in the early autumn garden, berries are hard to beat. Hips of species roses such as *Rosa moyesii*, *R. rubrifolia* and *R. rugosa* are at their peak now, while cotoneasters, barberries, pyracanthas and pernettyas are also coming into fruit. All look magnificent set against a backdrop of yellowing leaves.

▼ **Autumn berries** The native spindle tree (*Euonymus europaeus*) bears a profusion of pinkish-red seed capsules that split open to reveal orange seeds. *Callicarpa japonica* offers a sunny contrast with its golden leaves that turn maroon before falling.

▶ **Autumn blaze** The fast-growing, self-clinging vine *Parthenocissus tricuspidata* turns through yellow to fiery red before falling. Ideal for covering unsightly walls, its bare stems are in winter hidden by the evergreen foliage of a trained firethorn (*Pyracantha* sp.) whose huge bunches of red, yellow or orange berries persist for months.

▼ **Autumn borders** *Sedum* 'Autumn Joy' is a favourite subject for early autumn colour. Its pink-red flowerheads and fleshy pale green leaves are here backed by the 2.1m (7ft) tall silky-flowered grass *Miscanthus sinensis* 'Silver Feather'. Vivid yellow is introduced with a clump of golden rod (*Solidago* 'Crown of Rays') and rich blue with the shrubby *Ceratostigma willmottianum*. A front edging of dark violet flower spikes (*Liriope muscari*) unites the display.

◄ **Pastel shades** At a time when summer's blooms are fading and wilting, others emerge to bring new life to the garden. Delicate pink *Nerine bowdenii,* which needs plenty of sun and shelter, is backed by the 90cm (3ft) high, lavender-blue *Aster × frikartii* set against a sea of soft pink — the saucer-shaped flowers of Japanese anemones (*Anemone × hybrida*). In the background, the dusky-pink lacecap heads of *Hydrangea villosa* are reaching towards their ultimate height of 2.1m (7ft).

▼ **Blue and yellow** Autumn repeats the popular colour combinations of spring. Ceanothus, deciduous or evergreen, bears dense panicles of blue flowers for much of the year, the variety 'Autumn Blue' in late summer and autumn. The deep blue flowers stand out against the yellowing leaves of other deciduous shrubs.

▲ **Pink and red** Dahlias herald the coming of autumn, with morning mists and falling leaves. In a wide range of shapes and colours, dahlias bloom for many weeks — here pink cactus dahlias tone down the burning colour of the bronze-red *Helenium autumnale* 'Moerheim Beauty'.

◄ **Rose hips** Species roses, such as this *Rosa moyesii*, have a special place in the autumn garden, with their large flask-shaped, orange-red hips. *Rosa moyesii* itself is a vigorous shrub reaching 3.6m (12ft), but smaller varieties, such as 'Geranium' are more suitable for the modest-sized garden. Purple-pink goblets of autumn crocus (*Colchicum speciosum*) make a handsome underplanting while the canary-yellow autumn leaves of the Japanese maple (*Acer palmatum* 'Senkaki') form a perfect backdrop to the scene; in winter this acer lives up to its common name of coral bark when its young branches glow vivid red.

▼ **Autumn cheer** Hardy cyclamens thrive and naturalize in the shade and shelter of trees. The autumn-flowering *Cyclamen hederifolium* spreads a delicate pink carpet over the ground amid variegated ivy foliage; its own silver-marbled leaves do not appear until the blooms are completely over.

IN DEEP MIDWINTER

**Braving rains and storms, frost and thaw,
bulbs, evergreen shrubs and flowering trees decorate
the winter garden with welcome colour.**

In the depth of winter it is easy to believe that the garden is asleep or dead. Unless, that is, some thought has gone into planning it for the dullest months of the year.

Quite a few shrubs stage a spectacular flowering display in winter, and the delicate blooms of deciduous trees look stunning against a background of evergreens in an infinite variety of green, gold and blue where shafts of pale winter sun illuminate them.

Colour in the winter garden has the greatest impact from massed displays. Plant groups of miniature bulbs near the house, beneath trees or at the front of beds and borders. The snowdrop is the first to appear, followed shortly by winter aconites, white, blue or pink *Anemone blanda*, early crocuses and dwarf bright blue, yellow or purple-blue and orange irises. Plant them in

drifts with tiny, pale yellow hoop petticoat narcissi (*Narcissus bulbocodium*) or golden *N. cyclamineus* whose shape is echoed in the hardy *Cyclamen coum* whose pink, rose or white flowers appear in January.

In an exceptionally mild year, the Christmas rose (*Helleborus niger*) blooms in December, followed later by the taller Lenten rose and the showy *H. corsicus* with clusters of yellow-green drooping flowers.

The rock garden comes alive in late winter with tiny, pale mauve-blue hepaticas that resemble wild anemones and with the pure white *Saxifraga burserana* and pink *S. × kewensis*. The miniature *Primula × juliana* also blooms in mid winter, with wine-red primrose flowers in the 'Wanda' strain, competing with the sturdy winter pansies that, flattened by rain and snow, rise again to continue a long display of bright

colours. With rigorous dead-heading, these biennials will go on for several months.

No winter garden should be without the sweet-scented daphnes and the long-flowering heathers. The easy mezereon (*Daphne mezereum*) is studded in late winter with purple-red flowers, darker than the evergreen and more tender but deliciously fragrant *D. odora*. The winter heathers (*Erica carnea*), tolerant of lime and happiest in full sun, spread carpets over the ground with pink, rosy-purple, red or white spikes set above green, golden or bronze foliage.

▼ **Winter sun** Harbinger of spring, *Adonis amurensis* 'Fukujakai' pokes bright yellow, bowl-shaped flowers and ferny foliage through a light covering of snow in late winter.

Conifers are perfect partners for winter-flowering trees, giving both background colour and wind protection for the delicate spider flowers of the witch hazels. *Hamamelis × intermedia* bears very large flowers with crimped and twisted yellow petals. The cultivar 'Jelena' is suffused with copper and 'Ruby Glow' with bright red. *H. mollis*, the most popular of the witch hazels, clusters the leafless branches with golden blooms, pale yellow and red-flushed in 'Pallida'. Both are as sweetly fragrant as the slightly tender wintersweet (*Chimonanthus praecox*) whose claw-shaped, lime-yellow flowers, appearing from Christmas on, are stained deep purple.

At this time, too, appear the first early camellias. Few shrubs can rival these evergreens in beauty and perfection of bloom. Mainly hardy and with handsome glossy foliage, early types in particular need the shelter of a wall. *C. japonica* is one of the earliest, with the cultivar 'Adolphe Audusson' being the first to unfold its semi-double scarlet blooms. Some varieties of *C. × williamsii* are just as early, like the single 'November Pink' and the silvery 'Donation', reputedly the finest camellia and like others in this group distinguished with attractive and prominent golden stamens.

The shrubby *Magnolia stellata* is slow-growing, but even young plants are smothered with white, star-shaped and scented flowers in late winter while the pale green leaf buds are still tightly curled up beneath downy scales.

▲ **February colour** The Lenten rose (*Helleborus orientalis*) has a mind of its own, producing red, pink, cream or white saucer-shaped flowers, the insides freckled with crimson.

Most heathers will grow in no other than acid soil, but one alpine species, *Erica carnea* (syn. *E. herbacea*) is quite happy on lime and begins flowering as early as November, its dense spikes of white, pink, red or purple bell flowers blooming without a break until April. Ericas are of compact habit and make good ground cover, up to 30cm (1ft) high with a spread of twice that, of neat foliage that is usually bright green but golden in the cultivar 'Aurea' and bronze in the red-flowered 'Vivellii'.

E. × darleyensis grows twice the height of its parent, *E. carnea*, and is equally lime-tolerant. Its 15cm (6in) long flower spikes are borne from December until May.

◀ **Pink and white** From autumn until late spring, the evergreen shrub *Viburnum tinus* is a constant delight. Pink in the bud, the flat flower heads open pure white amid dark green foliage, assets prized by all flower arrangers.

▲ **Shades of green** The evergreen, quick-growing *Garrya elliptica* assumes tree proportions against a sunny wall. Magnificent in its full winter glory, it begins to produce lime-green flowers already in late summer; by mid winter it is wreathed in a mass of drooping catkins as much as 25cm (10in) long that last for several months. In sheltered regions, it makes an eye-catching specimen tree for the open garden.

◄ **Winter cheer** Undaunted by weather, *Erica carnea* blooms throughout winter and spring, spreading its neat evergreen hummocks as cheerful ground cover among dwarf conifers and fronting shrub borders. Dozens of named varieties range in colour from purest white to deep purple and repay an annual clipping in late spring with ever more brilliant displays the following winter.

The majority of rhododendrons flower during the spring months, but a few brighten the winter scene, such as the pink and white 'Christmas Cheer' and the rose-red 'Praecox'. All early-flowering shrubs need careful siting, in sunny or lightly shaded positions sheltered from strong winds. Avoid east-facing sites where morning sun after night frost can easily scorch buds and open flowers.

Prunus species are less spectacular but also less finicky. Earliest of all is *P. subhirtella* 'Autumnalis', the Higan cherry, which begins flowering in late autumn and bears semi-double white or pink flowers well into spring at the merest touch of the weak spring sun.

Early-flowering forms of *P. incisa*, the Fuji cherry, can be seen at the same time. 'Praecox' is the earliest, opening from pink buds to white blooms, often overlapping with the pale pink 'February Pink'.

▼ **Winter colonies** The bare-stemmed pale mauve goblets of *Crocus tomasinianus* unfold at the sun's caress to reveal deeper purple interiors. Left to their own devices, in unmown grass or beneath trees, these February-flowering crocuses spread steadily to form clumps.

▲ **Sunshine yellow** No need to pamper the ultra-hardy winter jasmine (*Jasminum nudiflorum*) for it flowers abundantly on even a cold north-facing wall, from late autumn to spring. The lax, dark green stems, though, need the support of trellis or wires.

▼ **White as snow** The snowdrop (*Galanthus nivalis*), poetically known as Fair Maid of February, grows wild in shady woodlands. Often taking a year or two to become established, the white bells cheerily ring out the passing of winter and the arrival of spring.

Leaf colours

Green is the basic gardening colour, the canvas on which all other colours are painted. In summer, when the garden is overflowing with brilliant colours and enticing scents, areas of foliage offer a restful pause. Many beautiful flowers fail to make their full impact because of a fussy background – foliage plants are essential companions to flowers, both as a backdrop and to complement them by their colour, their shape, or their size.

And during the long winter months when the garden is usually at its dreariest, leaves – both the usual shades of green and the more unexpected silvers, purples and yellows – come into their own. The colours, shapes and textures of evergreen foliage bring interest and life to the barren winter garden.

Leaves needn't be boring. They come in many shades, from pale lime to dark olive, from shimmering silver to rich purple. Leaves can be as large as dinner plates, or as tiny as finger nails. Some are divided into a lacy pattern; others grow in bolder shapes. They can be flecked, spotted, streaked or edged with contrasting shades of green; they can be variegated with white, yellow, gold, pink or bronze.

And while evergreen leaves maintain the same interest all year round, some deciduous leaves change with the seasons: unfolding palest green or pink, and maturing to darker shades. In autumn, they may take on brilliant hues of crimson, bronze, yellow or gold.

Silver and grey A sombre corner is brightened with artemisias, grasses and lavenders.

PEACEFUL GREENS

**Contrasting shades, shapes and textures of
green leaves can create as much pleasure as a palette
of bright colours in the garden.**

All too often, gardeners concentrate their thoughts on brightly coloured flowers at the expense of green foliage. But green leaves are the most important element of any garden: they last longer than the flowers and they are also what makes the garden a calm, peaceful place in which to rest. It pays to think carefully about the grouping of these green-leaved plants – choose a selection that offers contrasting shades of green as well as different leaf textures, shapes and growth habits.

Green plants come in an enormous range of hues – dark green, mid-green, grey-green, blue-green and yellow-green – so introducing colour variety is not difficult. Bear in mind that these greens have different qualities. Blue-green, for example, is a cool, receding colour which will give an arrangement depth, while yellow-green stands out, introducing welcome relief to the more sombre shades; a variegated species, such as *Euonymus fortunei*, is particularly useful.

Try and avoid grouping together plants with similar-sized leaves. Large expanses of uniformly small leaves can look tedious without the interruption of bold, large-leaved plants, and an association of big-leaved plants will appear both clumsy and boring without smaller foliage.

A variety of leaf textures adds further interest to an all-green grouping. Smooth, rough, hairy, and glossy surfaces reflect light in different ways, thus affecting the visual colour of the plants.

Consider also the growth habit of your foliage plants – the way the branches grow and how the leaves are arranged. Box, cypress and junipers, for example, have closely packed leaves and branches which give an overall impression of a dense, solid shape. To have an association composed just of these species – even if their leaves come in contrasting colours and textures – would be most uninspiring. But if you intersperse them with plants of a more open habit, which

allow shafts of sunlight to penetrate, creating patterns of light and shade, a more pleasing picture is produced.

To make a feature of your leafy green association include at least one foliage plant that catches the eye. Sculpture plants with their dramatic leaves and form are ideal for this. In a shady or semi-shaded site, ornamental rhubarb (*Rheum*) never fails to be noticed, partly because of its size but also because of the boldness of its leaves. If you're looking for something on a smaller scale, *Iris foetidissima*, whose clumps of dark leaves rise like a cluster of swords, is a good choice.

▼ **Evergreen foliage** Year-round colour and sculptural interest is achieved in this small and sheltered town garden with a spiky-leaved palm (*Chamaerops excelsa*) mirrored in the pool. At the far wall, a hand-shaped glossy-leaved *Fatsia japonica* towers above a clump of sword-shaped New Zealand flax (*Phormium tenax*).

◄ **Green and white** The gracefully arching, variegated leaves of *Hosta fortunei* 'Albopicta' form the centrepiece in this green and white partnership for dappled shade. They are backed by 90cm (3ft) tall stems of the annual, green-flowered love-lies-bleeding (*Amaranthus caudatus* 'Viridis') and partnered by pure white spikes of *Antirrhinum* 'White Spire'.

▼ **Green carpets** Low foliage plants, such as the heart-shaped spotted lungwort (*Pulmonaria saccharata*) and the red-tinted barrenwort (*Epimedium* × *rubrum*), spread a luxuriant carpet over moist and cool soil. In summer, the perennial grass *Hakonechloa macra* 'Albo-aurea' makes a stunning contrast in colour and form, and in autumn and winter the leaves of barrenwort turn the carpet into shades of blazing orange and yellow that persist until the following spring.

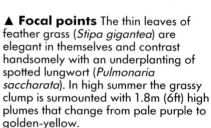

▲ **Focal points** The thin leaves of feather grass (*Stipa gigantea*) are elegant in themselves and contrast handsomely with an underplanting of spotted lungwort (*Pulmonaria saccharata*). In high summer the grassy clump is surmounted with 1.8m (6ft) high plumes that change from pale purple to golden-yellow.

◄ **Leafy contrasts** Well developed long before the flowers appear in late summer and autumn, the rough-textured vine-like foliage of *Anemone* × *hybrida* contrasts effectively with the dainty soft green fronds of the oak fern (*Gymnocarpium dryopteris*). This thrives in moist cool conditions and enjoys the company of meadowsweet (*Filipendula ulmaria* 'Aurea') whose gold foliage and cream flowers add a shaft of light.

► **Green upon green** This display maintains colour and interest throughout the year. At the back a 1.8m (6ft) tall Himalayan honeysuckle (*Leycesteria formosa*) decorates its arching stems in summer with drooping racemes of white flowers surrounded by purple bracts. They are followed by black-purple berries and, in late autumn, by purple leaves that fall to reveal bright green winter stems, the same colour as the twiggy shoots of *Kerria japonica* in front. The bare stems of these shrubs are ideal partners for a dense planting of the evergreen *Helleborus lividus corsicus* whose lime-green flowers are borne from late winter on, to be joined in spring by white spikes of *Bergenia* 'Silberlicht' and golden button flowers of the kerria.

▲ Evergreen shelter A background of conifers shelters the young leaves of *Acer japonicum* 'Aureum' from cold winds and sun scorch. Maturing to soft yellow, they then turn almost crimson in autumn, beautifully illuminated by the steel-blue soft foliage of a false cypress (*Chamaecyparis pisifera* 'Boulevard').

▶ Large-scale greenery Space is needed for this magnificent group whose centrepiece is the tree-like *Rhododendron calophytum*. Established specimens flower in spring, with large clusters of white and purple blooms, but the true glory lies in the appearance of new leaves that unfold as silvery shuttlecocks sheathed in purple-brown scales above the 'umbrellas' of more mature leaves.

Such striking foliage demands similar companions — the backing of a blue-leaved spruce (*Picea pungens glauca*) and, as a footing, the golden-green shuttlecock fronds of the ostrich-feather fern (*Matteuccia struthiopteris*). As complete contrasts, plant in front the perennial foliage plant *Peltiphyllum peltatum* with huge wheel-like leaves, the graceful blue-green *Hosta sieboldiana* 'Elegans' and *Rodgersia aesculifolia* from whose rosettes of chestnut-like leaves rise airy summer spikes of creamy flowers.

SILVER AND GREY FOLIAGE

**Use grey and silver foliage plants alone or
as companions for pastel pinks and blues, to form
shimmering pools of light in the garden.**

Silver and grey foliage plants have two great assets – their delicate colour and their soft velvety texture which comes from the thin covering of hairs they have developed to help them withstand drought and survive the hot conditions of their native lands.

Grey and silver all-foliage plants bring relief to a jungle of green leaves and offer contrasting textures. You could also add a variegated species with silver markings to provide a link between the greens and silvers, so binding the planting together.

Several different silver foliage species can look extremely effective grown together, as long as you make sure they are not too similar. Select plants for their varying leaf shapes and different growth habits. *Eryngium giganteum*, with its thistle-like flowerheads and spiky bracts, is an excellent plant to bear in mind. It draws attention to any all-silver grouping with its elegant form.

If you can't resist some flower colour, pale pinks and blues mix with the greys and silvers to add a touch of warmth without being too strident. White, too, is a most distinguished companion – it enhances a border of silver foliage plants to make a glistening sea of reflecting light. Good candidates are *Gypsophila paniculatus*, perennial phlox and stately, pure white delphiniums.

▼ **White and silver** Clumps of white flowers – daisy-like *Osteospermum ecklonis* (front), *Chrysanthemum maximum* and the narrow spikes of *Veronica virginica* 'Alba' (back) – highlight the grey and silver foliage plants in this herbaceous summer border.

◄ **Shady ground covers** The dead nettle (*Lamium maculatum*) and lamb's tongue (*Stachys lanata*) are perfect ground cover companions — the dead nettle's distinctive silver markings reflect the velvety grey-white leaves of the lamb's tongue and together they create shafts of light over shady ground. Dead nettle flowers from late spring through summer and into autumn, with white flowers in the cultivar 'Album' and shell-pink in 'Roseum'.

◄ Silver light The pure white globes of the spider flower (*Cleome hasslerana* 'Helen Campbell') hold centre stage in this summer tapestry of silver, grey and white. A half-hardy annual, the spider flower is particularly suitable as a dot or accent plant among equally tall neighbours, such as the white-tasselled *Lysimachia clethroides* and steel-blue *Eryngium giganteum* with silvery, spiny bracts. A shimmering silver sea of wormwood (*Artemisia absinthium* 'Valerie Finnis') provides the perfect backdrop and the ferny silver-grey foliage of *Senecio maritimus* creates pools of light in the foreground.

► Cool in summer Slender, soft blue English irises (*Iris xiphioides*) rise above a froth of *Senecio maritimus* whose silver-blue ferny foliage will camouflage the dying iris leaves after the summer flowering.

► Foliage schemes
Enchanting silver and grey foliage plants cluster round an evergreen cider gum tree (*Eucalyptus gunnii*), whose blue-green leaves preside over the sprawling grey-felted *Senecio* 'Sunshine' with leaf undersides that are shimmering white. Blue is repeated in a foreground planting of the ground-hugging *Hebe pinguifolia* 'Pagei' and in the strategic placing of a clump of spring-flowering *Allium albopilosum* whose blue flower globes turn to dusky brown seed heads by late summer.

◄ **Silver frames** The finely dissected foliage of *Senecio maritimus* surrounds a pastel-coloured group of everlasting annuals – *Helipterum roseum* with pink flowers and *H. manglesii* with red and white daisy blooms. At the front tumble old-fashioned, sweetly-scented pinks (*Dianthus* 'White Ladies').

▼ **Pure silver** A shrubby *Centaurea gymnocarpa* 'Colchester White' arches its silver-white, lacy leaf fronds above low-growing but wide-spreading *Tanacetum haradjanii* (sometimes listed as *T. densum* 'Amani'). Its elegant feathery foliage is topped in late summer with dense clusters of yellow, groundsel-like flowers.

GOLDEN FOLIAGE PLANTS

**On their own, or as a complement
to flowers, golden foliage plants bring
light to any garden.**

Golden and golden-variegated foliage plants look cheering against green or grey foliage, are especially effective in shady corners, give a warm feeling of spring, and make excellent cuttings for flower arranging. They can bring a splash of yellow where yellow flowers might not grow, or provide undiluted colour on a much larger scale than flowers could ever do.

The category includes a wide range of hues, from pale, creamy yellow to deepest gold. Unlike the various shades of red, yellows harmonize naturally and different shades can be planted next to each other without clashing.

Variegated golden foliage comes in many forms. It can be splashed, striped, spotted, edged or softly suffused with yellow, and combines well with green, white, grey, pink, purple and mixtures of these colours.

Textures vary also. Golden elaeagnus and holly, for example, are shiny and reflective, while the golden, moss-like *Sagina glabra* 'Aurea' is velvety and light-absorbing. Thus, a cheerful floral effect can be created without a single flower.

Using yellow

Yellow behaves like white, drawing the eye with its luminosity – the darker the background, the more luminous yellow appears. It is especially powerful in the late afternoon and evening, when darker colours start to fade. Unlike white, however, yellow never appears flat or 'bleached out', even in strong midday sun. These properties make it a natural focal point – so use it with care. As a general rule, yellow looks better planted in single, large splashes or bold groups and backgrounds than when it is scattered about.

Golden foliage can be used to brighten dark corners, giving a

▼ **Sunshine yellow** As a focal point in light shade, try *Acer japonicum* 'Aureum' whose soft yellow leaf canopy fans outs symmetrically. In full sun, the foliage may scorch.

▲ **Gold rush** Ornamental forms of such culinary herbs as mint and marjoram spread quickly to form dense ground covers. They need full sun in order to retain the golden variegations.

▼ **Bamboo screens** The vivid yellow and green-striped foliage of the clump-forming bamboo *Arundinaria viridistriata* brings a vivid burst of sunlight to a shady spot.

▲ **Autumn yellow** *Acer palmatum* 'Senkaki' positively glows against a dark background in autumn. In winter, the young branches live up to the common name of coral bark maple.

feeling of lightness where little light actually reaches. Golden hops and golden-variegated ivy positively glow in the dark.

Golden foliage – particularly evergreens – can provide a longer-lasting display than yellow flowers, something that is an important attribute in winter, when flowers (of any colour) and sunshine are in short supply. It also provides contrasting form and texture in borders or beds of green foliage, and shows up especially well against a dark background, such as a yew hedge.

Golden foliage makes a decorative edging or hedge in its own right. While golden or variegated box is ideal for a low, formal clipped hedge, golden yew is the answer for a hedge on a grander scale. Low-growing sprawling plants, such as creeping Jenny (*Lysimachia nummularia* 'Aurea') or golden thyme (*Thymus* × *citriodorus* 'Aureus') make a pleasing bright informal edging. Marbled hedging or edging – mixing gold and plain green plants – is a lovely tradition, but the stronger-growing green plants must be prevented from swamping the slower-growing yellow ones.

Golden-foliage plants make excellent eye-catching ground cover: golden heather (*Calluna vulgaris* 'Gold Haze' and *Erica carnea* 'Aurea'), golden lemon balm (*Melissa officinalis* 'Aurea'), golden creeping Jenny, various golden grasses – and even the much maligned, somewhat taller, yellow-splashed and spotted laurel (*Aucuba japonica* 'Maculata'), which flourishes in the darkest corner and fills space where almost nothing else will grow.

Golden-foliaged plants with large scale or bold foliage attract attention immediately. A tree on a lawn, or a dwarf conifer in a rockery, are natural specimen plants. For summer bedding schemes, there is golden-leaved coleus (*Coleus blumei*), golden feverfew (*Chrysanthemum parthenium*), variegated busy Lizzie (*Impatiens holstii*) and, for an impressive dot plant, the variegated ornamental maize (*Zea mays* 'Quadricolor'). There are also tender fuchsias with golden or golden-variegated leaves and the familiar golden-leaved zonal pelargoniums – 'Mrs Quilter', 'Mrs Henry Cox', 'Happy Thought', 'Golden Harry Hieover', to name

▲ **Golden balm** The fragrant, green and gold leaves of *Melissa officinalis* 'Aureum' offer decorative ground cover. Prune the plants in early summer to encourage variegations.

but a few – whose foliage is every bit as attractive as their flowers.

Ways with gold

Golden foliage can be part of an all-foliage scheme or mixed with flowers. For an entirely gold or golden-variegated bed, choose plants with a range of form and structure, heights, leaf shapes and sizes. Try to have a mixture of evergreen and deciduous plants for year-round interest.

Plant golden-variegated shrubs and perennials in bold drifts. If they are small, set three, five or seven plants of a single type in a clump. Separate different species of variegated plants with areas of solid-colour planting, otherwise the effect can be overwhelming.

▼ **Cascades of gold** The fast-growing *Sambucus racemosa* 'Plumosa Aurea' fills a shady corner with light and grace. Hard pruning of all side shoots in spring results in fresh luxuriant foliage.

▶ **Purple and gold** The fast-growing evergreen *Elaeagnus* × *ebbingei* 'Gilt Edge' is a marvellous garden shrub, its leathery leaves tolerating wind and sea sprays. It shines like a beacon in shady areas throughout the year, catching and reflecting the natural light that the sombre hues of purple foliage absorb.

▼ **Yellow creepers** The golden creeping Jenny (*Lysimachia nummularia* 'Aurea') trails its leafy stems as happily over stony edgings as over waterside banks. The small bright yellow evergreen leaves are a cheerful addition to taller ground covers of variegated dead nettle (*Lamium maculataum*) and grey-green lavender.

PURPLE FOLIAGE

Planted with imagination and discipline, purple foliage brings depth, drama and contrast to otherwise plain plant partnerships.

Purple foliage, tinted bronze, copper, red or so deeply coloured that it approaches black, brings richness and excitement to the garden – but it is so dominant that it should be used sparingly.

There are many beautiful purple-foliaged plants to choose from. Use them to soften flowers with hot flame colours – or, if the purple foliage seems too harsh, harmonizing bright blues, violets and soft pinks will tone it down. White and yellow offer vivid contrasts – plant pale yellow with dark purples and dark yellows with light purples for the greatest impact. For foliage scenes partner purple-leaved plants with grey, yellow or white variegations.

For example, a purple carpet of *Sedum spathulifolium* 'Purpureum' in a sunny rock garden would be perfectly complemented throughout the year by the grey-leaved form *S. s.* 'Cape Blanco'; in spring yellow crocuses could provide a stunning colour contrast.

In semi-shade 60cm (2ft) high Bowles' golden grass (*Milium effusum* 'Aureum') gives height and colour definition to a planting of mid green, purple-suffused *Viola labradorica* 'Purpurea'.

At the front of a border in early summer, the upright, creamy yellow flower spikes of *Sisyrinchium striatum* are perfect companions for the large purple leaves of plantain (*Plantago major* 'Purpurea'). The white cups of *Campanula poscharskyana* 'Alba' provide a further light contrast which emphasizes the purple.

▲ **Purple and blue** Rich purple suffuses the fleshy leaves of stonecrop (*Sedum maximum* 'Atropurpureum') and extends to the autumn flower heads. Purple, too, is the colour in the flower bracts of stately *Acanthus spinosus* toned down with lavender-blue *Aster* × *frikartii*.

▼ **Royal purple** The deep purple leaves of *Cotinus coggygria* 'Royal Purple' are almost translucent in bright sun; in autumn they turn glowing red before falling.

◄ **Autumn splendour**
The huge palmate leaves and dusky brown seed heads of the purple castor oil plant (*Ricinus communis* 'Gibsonii') tower above flat-topped wine-red *Sedum* 'Autumn Joy' and slender purple-blue spikes of *Salvia farinacea*. A clump of gardener's garters (*Phalaris arundinacea* 'Picta') lends a touch of lightness with its green and white-striped grassy leaves.

► **Purple and silver** The silky, finely divided leaves of silvery white *Artemisia absinthium* 'Lambrook Silver', a much improved form of the native wormwood, link a purple planting of *Sedum maximum* 'Atropurpureum' with the strongly fragrant, red and white-striped Gallica rose 'Versicolor'.

▲ **Summer exotics** Dramatic in colour, shape and texture, the tender purple-leaved *Canna* × *generalis* is here bedded out with rose-pink mallows (*Lavatera trimestris*) and lavender-purple petunias. The annuals can be left to complete their life cycle outdoors, but the canna must be brought under cover before autumn.

◄ **Spring companions** The striking bronze-crimson foliage of the Japanese maple (*Acer palmatum* 'Atropurpureum') gives an almost theatrical depth to the soft pink flowers of *Daphne* × *burkwoodii* 'Somerset' in late spring. Variegated hostas at the front thrive in the dappled shade and moist soil.

▲ Foliage for flower arrangers
The purple forms of the smoke tree (*Cotinus coggygria*) with its pale purple, feathery flower plumes in summer belong in every flower arranger's repertoire. In the garden, the purple leaves associate brilliantly with the white-variegated dogwood (*Cornus alba* 'Elegantissima').

► Bedding partners
The ordinary fennel (*Foeniculum vulgare*) is a most decorative herb, especially in the form 'Atropurpureum' which bears yellow flower heads in late summer. The bronze foliage echoes the purple-leaved, scarlet-flowered dahlias in a scheme lightened with white *Lavatera trimestris* 'Mont Blanc' on one side and the soft pink of the Hybrid tea rose 'Madame Butterfly' on the other.

YEAR ROUND LEAF COLOURS

**Foliage is the most important element
in the garden picture, providing background and
accent points throughout the seasons.**

Evergreen trees and shrubs bring beauty to the garden all the year round, clothing it in colour when flowers have gone underground and deciduous trees and shrubs stand bare. Many, like camellias and the Mexican orange have wonderful floral displays, but when these have finished, the foliage continues to furnish an attractive background colour. Others, such as all the laurels (*Aucuba* sp.), evergreen spindle trees (*Euonymus fortunei* and *E. japonicus*) and the popular *Elaeagnus pungens* are insignifi-

cant in flower but invaluable for their foliage.

Green is the basic foliage colour but it comes in subtle variations and is often marked or flushed with other colours. The green pigmentation also differs according to the time of year, palest as the young leaves unfold in spring and, in deciduous trees and shrubs, darkening through the summer to coloured autumn tints.

Deciduous foliage plants should be selected carefully, and ideally have more than temporary interest. Trees like the birches and

acers delight with handsome winter bark and a delicate tracery of bare branches even when shorn of their leaves.

▼ **Autumn blaze** Shortening days, warm sun and cool nights trigger a chemical process in certain leaves that turns them from green to yellow and shades of bronze and red. The Japanese maples (*Acer palmatum*) are noted for their brilliant autumn colours and none more so than the cultivar 'Osakazuki'. Its fiery crimson autumn dress is enhanced by the deep golden-bronze foliage of *Fothergilla major*.

▲ **Colour accents** A conifer planting, displaying a diversity of shapes and colours against a background of deciduous trees, explodes in startling autumn fire where the sun illuminates foliage of brilliant red. The same colour is retained for months by the berries of *Cotoneaster horizontalis* at the front.

▶ **Scarlet and orange** The rapidly growing Virginia creeper (*Parthenocissus quinquefolia*) attaches itself to high house walls and trees, clothing them in large, handsome, five-fingered leaves. In autumn, they gradually turn from dark green to a vertical blaze of bronze and crimson before fluttering to the ground.

◀ **Autumn symphony** Ornamental crab apples are ideal trees for the small garden. Some are grown for their spring blossom or colourful fruit; others, like *Malus tschonoskii*, for their attractive shape and brilliant autumn tints. Cone-shaped when mature, this crab apple looks spectacular in a shrub border, transforming itself in autumn into a flaming torch of yellow and orange, bronze and purple before going out in crimson glory.

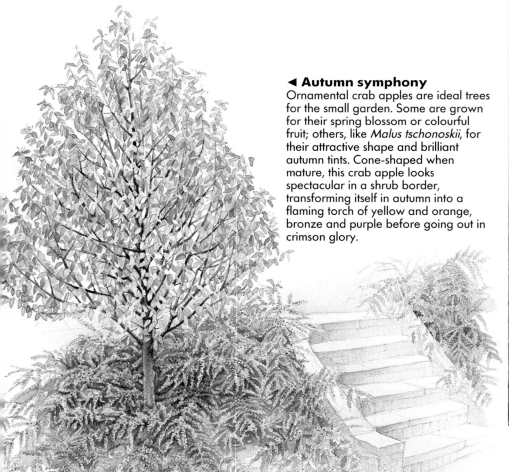

▲ **Frosted foliage** The winter garden becomes a magical fairyland where overnight frost has crisped the grassy clumps of red-hot pokers and ground-hugging rose of Sharon (*Hypericum calycinum*) with icy fingers. Above, the arching branches of *Berberis thunbergii* are still laden with bright red berries.

◄ **Silver firs** Most *Abies* species are too tall for the average garden, but the Korean fir (*A. koreana*) is slow-growing enough to suit even a shrub border. In winter, the silvery undersides of the needles glisten against the erect cones that change in colour from violet-purple to brown-black as they mature.

◄ **Evergreen spring** The blue Colorado spruce (*Picea pungens glauca*) raises its tiers of horizontal branches above a sprawling juniper busily extending arching shoots with young, fresh, green spring growth.

▼ **Gold and silver** Evergreen foliage associations retain their interest through the year. With the onset of bright spring light, the variegations of such shrubs as *Euonymus fortunei* 'Emerald and Gold' (left) and 'Silver Queen' (centre) increase in intensity.

▲ **Late spring** Warm sunshine brings out the flame-red variegations in the sword-shaped leaves of *Phormium tenax* 'Sundowner'. The evergreen clumps, which in sheltered gardens can reach as much as 3m (10ft) in height, cast a wide umbrella of dappled shade beneath which spring primulas thrive and prosper.

▲ **Summer foliage** Purple leaves can be difficult to accommodate among the strong flower colours of summer. The almost strident hues of the deciduous shrub *Berberis thunbergii* 'Rose Glow' are deep purple by midsummer and need the relief of a silvery-white underplanting such as *Euonymus fortunei* 'Silver Queen'.

▼ **Shrub borders** Lush green lawns circle curving borders of foliage plants punctuated with flowering summer perennials and edged with the brilliant tones of golden marjoram. The soft grey-green shoots of a broom contrast pleasantly with the deciduous, purple-leaved *Berberis thunbergii* 'Atropurpureum'.

▲ **Colour contrasts** In summer, the coral flower (*Heuchera*) is topped with dainty sprays of creamy-white bead-like flowers. The heart-shaped leaves, deep purple in 'Palace Purple', are evergreen and make marvellous edges for herbaceous and shrub borders. Here their sombre colour contrasts effectively with the silver-spotted foliage of lungwort (*Pulmonaria saccharata*).

▲ **Silver leaves** Foliage plants are rarely distinguished by their flowers. One exception is the summer-blooming sea holly (*Eryngium maritimum*) whose steel-blue flower heads, surrounded by spiny bracts, are as attractive as the silver-grey, finely cut foliage. This contrasts well with a footing of velvety lamb's tongue (*Stachys lanata*) whose purple-blue flower spikes are of little interest and best removed.

◀ **Foliage tapestry** Contrasting leaf colours, shapes and textures are combined in a successful partnership. Colour variations are provided by a purple-leaved prunus, a golden and green *Euonymus japonicus* 'Ovatus Aureus' and a pink-tinted *Spiraea* × *bumalda* 'Goldflame'. A dwarf pine (*Pinus mugo*) and a gold-tipped false cypress introduce different leaf textures while the graceful *Fuchsia magellanica* interrupts the solidity of the association.

TREES AND SHRUBS WITH OUTSTANDING LEAF COLOURS

	NAME	DESCRIPTION	HEIGHT	SITE
GOLDEN AND YELLOW FOLIAGE	Acer japonicum 'Aureum'	Deciduous, slow-growing; palmate leaves	3m (10ft)	Moist soil; shade/shelter
	Calluna vulgaris vars.	Evergreen; summer-autumn flowering	45cm (1½ft)	Lime-free soil; sun
	Catalpa bignonioides 'Aurea'	Deciduous; foxglove flowers, seed pods	6m (20ft)	Deep soil; shelter, sun
	Chamaecyparis obtusa 'Nana Aurea'	Dwarf, compact conifer; slow-growing	30cm (1ft)	Well-drained soil, sun
	Choisya ternata 'Sundance'	Evergreen; scented white flowers	90cm (3ft)	Any soil; sun/shelter
	Cornus alba 'Aurea'	Deciduous, fast-growing; red winter stems	3m (10ft)	Moist soil; sun/shade
	Corylus avellana 'Aurea'	Deciduous; winter catkins	3m (10ft)	Well-drained soil; sun
	Cupressus macrocarpa 'Goldcrest'	Narrow, upright conifer	90cm (3ft)	Well-drained soil; sun/shelter
	Euonymus japonicus 'Ovatus Aureus'	Deciduous, slow-growing, compact	90cm (3ft)	Any soil; sun or shade
	Gleditsia triacanthos 'Sunburst'	Deciduous, slow-growing; seed-pods	10m (30ft)	Well-drained soil; sun
	Larus nobilis 'Aurea'	Evergreen; withstands clipping	1.5m (5ft)	Any soil; sun/shelter
	Lonicera nitida 'Baggesen's Gold'	Evergreen; suitable for hedging	1.2m (4ft)	Any soil; sun
	Philadelphus coronarius 'Aureus'	Deciduous; creamy flowers in summer	1.8m (6ft)	Any soil; light shade
	Ribes sanguineum 'Brocklebankii'	Deciduous; pink spring flowers	1.2m (4ft)	Any soil; light shade
	Robinia pseudoacacia 'Frisia'	Deciduous; furrowed bark	12m (40ft)	Any soil; sun/shelter
	Sambucus racemosa 'Plumosa Aurea'	Deciduous, spreading; cream flowers	2.5m (8ft)	Moist soil; light shade
	Taxus baccata 'Semperaurea'	Dwarf conifer; slow-growing	90cm (3ft)	Well-drained soil; sun
	Thuja occidentalis 'Rheingold'	Dwarf conifer; slow-growing	90cm (3ft)	Any soil; full sun
	Vibernum opulus 'Aureum'	Deciduous, compact; summer-flowering	1.8m (6ft)	Moist soil; light shade
SILVER AND GREY/BLUE FOLIAGE	Abies concolor 'Glauca Compacta'	Dwarf conifer, slow-growing, compact	90cm (3ft)	Moist acid soil; sun
	Buddleia alternifolia 'Argentea'	Deciduous; arching; blue flowers	3m (10ft)	Rich soil; sun
	Chamaecyparis pisifera 'Boulevard'	Silver-blue dwarf conifer	90cm (3ft)	Well-drained soil; light shade
	Cytisus battandieri	Deciduous, upright; golden flowers	3m (10ft)	Poor soil; full sun
	Elaeagnus angustifolia	Deciduous, fast-growing; silvery blooms	4.5m (15ft)	Any soil; full sun
	Eucalyptus gunnii	Deciduous, fast-growing; stool annually	1.5m (5ft)	Moist soil; full sun
	Hebe pinguifolia 'Pagei'	Evergreen, wide-spreading; white flowers	15-23cm (6-9in)	Any soil; sun/shelter
	Helianthemum nummularium 'The Bride'	Evergreen, spreading; white flowers	15cm (6in)	Any soil; full sun
	Helichrysum petiolatum	Half-hardy; trailing stems	45cm (1½ft)	Well-drained soil; sun/shelter
	Juniperus 'Grey Owl'	Dwarf prostrate conifer, spreading	60cm (2ft)	Any soil; sun
	Lavandula angustifolia	Evergreen, aromatic; summer-flowering	60cm (2ft)	Any soil; sun
	Picea pungens glauca vars.	Slow-growing conifers	6m (20ft)	Moist acid soil; sun
	Pyrus salicifolia 'Pendula'	Deciduous; weeping	5.5m (18ft)	Rich soil; sun
	Salix repens 'Argentea'	Deciduous, prostrate or standard; catkins	90-180cm (3-6ft)	Moist soil; full sun
	Santolina chamaecyparissus	Evergreen; sprawling	75cm (2½ft)	Any soil; full sun
	Senecio 'Sunshine'	Evergreen; sprawling; yellow flowers	90cm (3ft)	Well-drained soil; sun
	Teucrium fruticans	Half-hardy; lavender-blue flowers	1.5m (5ft)	Poor soil; sun/shelter

	NAME	DESCRIPTION	HEIGHT	SITE
PURPLE AND RED FOLIAGE	Acer palmatum vars.	Deciduous shrubs and small trees	4.5m (15ft)	Moist soil; shelter/light shade
	Berberis thunbergii vars.	Deciduous, compact; yellow flowers	1.2m (4ft)	Any soil; sun/light shade
	Betula pendula 'Purpurea'	Deciduous, slow-growing; weeping	3m (10ft)	Loamy soil; sun/light shade
	Corylus maxima 'Purpurea'	Deciduous; yellow winter catkins	3m (10ft)	Any soil: sun/light shade
	Cotinus coggygria 'Royal Purple'	Deciduous; purple flowers in summer	2.4m (8ft)	Any soil; sun
	Euonymus europaeus 'Atropurpureum'	Deciduous; autumn tints and berries	1.8m (6ft)	Any soil; sun/light shade
	Malus x purpurea, M. 'Royalty'	Deciduous, spring flowering; fruit	4.5m (15ft)	Well-drained soil; sun
	Nandina domestica 'Nana Purpurea'	Half-hardy evergreen; white flowers	90cm (3ft)	Rich soil; sun/shelter
	Osmanthus heterophyllus 'Purpureus'	Evergreen, slow-growing; autumn flowers	1.8m (6ft)	Any soil; sun/shelter
	Phormium tenax 'Purpureum'	Evergreen; semi-hardy; sword-shaped	90cm (3ft)	Moist soil; sun/shelter
	Pittosporum tenuifolium 'Purpureum'	Evergreen, near hardy; flowers in May	3m (10ft)	Rich soil; sun/shelter
	Prunus x cistena, P. cerasifera vars.	Deciduous; spring-flowering	1.8m-6m (6-20ft)	Well-drained soil; sun
	Sambucus nigra 'Purpurea'	Deciduous; slow-growing	3m (10ft)	Moist soil; light shade or sun
	Viburnum tinus 'Purpureum'	Evergreen; winter-flowering	2.1m (7ft)	Moist soil, sun or light shade
	Vitis vinifera 'Purpurea'	Deciduous climber; autumn tints	15m (50ft)	Well-drained soil; sun/light shade
	Weigela florida 'Foliis Purpureis'	Deciduous, slow-growing; pink flowers	1.2cm (4ft)	Well-drained soil; sun
AUTUMN COLOURS (all deciduous)	Amelanchier species	Fast-growing; spring flowers	3m (10ft)	Moist soil; sun
	Carpinus betulus	Fast-growing; yellow tints	to 9m (30ft)	Any soil and site
	Ceratostigma willmottianum	Half-hardy; blue flowers, red foliage	90cm (3ft)	Well-drained soil; sun/shelter
	Cotoneaster horizontalis	Orange-crimson foliage and fruits	60cm (2ft)	Any soil; sun
	Euonymus alatus 'Compactus'	Red leaves, red/orange berries	1.8m (6ft)	Any soil; sun or light shade
	Fothergilla monticolor	Slow-growing; rich crimson tints	1.2m (4ft)	Acid soil; full sun
	Larix species	Deciduous conifers; golden/russet	to 18m (60ft)	Moist soil; sun
	Liquidambar styraciflua	Imposing tree; brilliant in autumn	10m (33ft)	Moist soil; sun or light shade
	Malus tschonoskii	White flowers; scarlet autumn foliage	6m (20ft)	Well-drained soil; sun
	Parrotia persica	Slow-growing; brilliant autumn tints	3m (10ft)	Well-drained soil; sun/light shade
	Parthenocissus quinquefolia	Vigorous climber; scarlet autumn leaves	15m (50ft)	Any soil; sun/light shade
	Pyracantha coccinea vars.	Evergreen; red, orange, yellow berries	2.4m (8ft)	Well-drained soil; sun/shade
	Rhus typhina	Suckering; superb autumn colours	5cm (17ft)	Any soil; sun
	Ribes odoratum	Fast-growing; yellow-orange in autumn	1.8m (6ft)	Well-drained soil; sun/shade
	Sorbaria aitchisonii	Suckering; autumn-flowering (cream)	1.8m (6ft)	Moist soil; sun/light shade
	Sorbus 'Joseph Rock'	Orange tints; yellow berries	6m (20ft)	Moist soil; sun
	Vaccinium corymbosum	Suckering; blue berries, red leaf tints	1.2m (4ft)	Moist acid soil; sun/light shade
	Viburnum latana	Red berries and autumn leaves	3m (10ft)	Any soil; sun/light shade
	Vitis coignetiae	Vigorous climber, rich autumn colours	15m (50ft)	Moist soil; sun

White and cream flowers

The art of putting plants together for maximum effect is largely a question of trial and error, and of personal taste. One person's joy is another's nightmare. Still, it can be a useful exercise to choose a basic favourite colour and experiment with other hues which harmonize or contrast with it. Many monochromatic schemes are splendid, as for example the famous White Garden which Vita Sackville-West created at Sissinghurst in Kent. Gardeners operating on more modest scales will content themselves with one or two pale-coloured arrangements that introduce areas of calm and tranquillity to the garden scene.

No colour is constant, and no colour exists at all without light. It changes from season to season and with the intensity of natural light, from morning to noon to night. White and pale cream colours are all but lost in the sharp early-morning light but come alive in late afternoon and at twilight. They are colours for placing against dark backgrounds, for separating vivid hues and for using at the far end of a small garden to make it appear larger than it is.

White is a luminous colour that increases the intensity of its surroundings; it mixes particularly well with the pastel shades of yellow, pink and blue flowers and with grey and silvery foliage. It can play the dominant partner in an association or the supporting role that brings sparkle to otherwise dull colours. Conversely, pure white can look clinical and stark next to such dark colours as purple and magenta though a blur of creamy blossom is not only complementary but also softens such hot colours.

White and cream At dusk, the colour of white flowers is the last to disappear.

WHITER THAN WHITE

Pure white flowers bring calm and freshness to the garden, illuminating it on dull days and prolonging interest after dusk.

White flowers tend to be used to separate plants with clashing colours or they are teamed with grey and silver foliage. However, such is the abundance of white-flowered plants – not forgetting white- or cream-variegated foliage – that you can create impressive plantings using them alone. And despite the use of only the single colour, the plantings are never monotonous for whites range from greyish to creamy and can be tinted pink, blue or green.

White flowers have other bonuses: they have a cooling effect on scorching hot days but light up the garden on a dull one; they gleam at dusk and stand out in moonlight when other colours vanish in the darkness.

So it's a good plan to have a group of summer-blooming white flowers by French windows where they can be seen from indoors at twilight, or by an outdoor seating area used on summer evenings.

You can create an attractive feature for mid to late spring by underplanting a silver birch with clumps of the bulb *Ornithogalum nutans*, which has spikes of drooping white flowers, green on the outside, held on 38cm (15in) stems. Partner it with the white form of snake's-head fritillary, *Fritillaria meleagris* 'Aphrodite', along with white-variegated hostas, whose foliage is particularly fresh at this time of year. Choose from *Hosta undulata*, with white or silvery markings, and *H. albomarginata* with white leaf edges. A drift of some of the last narcissi to flower, the gently fragrant *Narcissus poeticus*, would complete this late spring picture.

In summer, the large-flowered clematis 'Marie Boisselot' or the smaller 'Huldine' make a beautiful backdrop for groups of white

cosmos and the double *Chrysanthemum maximum* 'Wirral Supreme'. For spiky contrast, use white delphiniums at the rear and *Campanula persicifolia* 'Alba' further forward. Small edging plants could include *Viola cornuta* 'Alba', scented, white-flowered pinks (*Dianthus* × *allwoodii*), sweet alyssum and *Campanula carpatica* 'Bressingham White'.

During late summer and early autumn, when a border might look a little tired, bring it to life with

the 1.2m (4ft) tall narrow spikes of *Veronica virginica* 'Alba' and the well-formed heads of *Phlox* 'White Admiral'. Add white Japanese anemones, whose large saucer-shaped blooms can be set off with the variegated leaves of the annual *Euphorbia marginata*. In turn, back these with the white-variegated foliage of *Cornus alba* 'Elegantissima' and finish with the cream flowers of *Clematis viticella* 'Alba Luxurians' for a delightful display.

► **White as snow** Gracefully tall and of the purest white, these delphiniums create a stunning vertical element in a mid summer border. They are backed with arching sprays of *Spiraea* × *arguta* 'The Bride' and a large-flowered, snow-white clematis.

▲ **Peaceful corners** On scorching summer days the eye rests with relief on a calm splash of white. In the centre of this scheme is a huge clump of long-spurred aquilegia hybrids above elegant foliage, their golden centres echoed in the tiny daisy flowers of erigerons at the base of a retaining wall. The foaming heads of *Centranthus ruber* 'Albus' will continue to shimmer against the dark green hedge long after its companions, the white spiky foxgloves, have finished flowering.

◄ **Summer freshness** In late summer, when strong flower colours have almost burnt themselves out, *Phlox paniculata* 'Snow Queen' dazzles with the purest white, the large dome-shaped flower heads persisting until early autumn. They contrast agreeably with *Lysimachia ephereum* whose airy flower spikes, as much as 30cm (1ft) tall, are held above narrow grey-green leaves.

◄ **Symbols of purity** The emblem of France and frequently included in religious paintings to symbolize innocence, the lily is indeed magnificent. *Lilium regale* is one of the easiest to grow; its tall stems are topped in mid summer with fragrant white trumpets, stained rosy-purple on the backs of the petals and with centres of prominent golden-yellow stamens. Here, it overshadows the flower clusters of the accommodating daisy bush (*Olearia × haastii*), which continues to bloom long after the lily has sounded its last trumpet.

▲ **Carpet of white** The evergreen candytuft *(Iberis sempervirens)* can spread its carpets of dark green leaves far and wide. In late spring and early summer it becomes dense drifts of white flowers stopped in midflow by a clump of *Hosta crispula* whose long-pointed, dark green leaves are strikingly edged with white.

▼ **Tender white** Blooming from mid summer to autumn, graceful *Gaura lindheimeri,* a 1.2m (4ft) tall perennial usually treated as an annual, makes an airy companion for two half-hardy annuals — *Cosmos* with bright green feathery foliage and large white flowers, and the white, pink-tinted spider flower *(Cleome spinosa).*

▲ **Mop heads of white** The Hortensia group of *Hydrangea macrophylla* has huge mop heads of sterile florets in white, red, pink or blue or combinations of these. Impressive as a late summer-flowering wall shrub, its sheer size is emphasized by a stone trough brimming with the modest but complementary *Calamintha nepetiodes.*

► **White bedders** The shrubby but half-hardy Paris daisy (*Chrysanthemum frutescens*) is particularly suitable for container-growing and for bedding in full sun. Its white daisy flowers and neat ferny foliage, grey-green and almost silvery, contrasts handsomely with the open funnels of white petunias. If regularly dead-headed, both will bloom throughout summer and into autumn; the Paris daisy can often be successfully overwintered under glass.

▼ **Semi wilderness** Majestic white foxgloves (*Digitalis purpurea* 'Alba') are dotted about in a semi-shaded woodland setting. Their 1.2m (4ft) tall stems hold the drooping tubular flowers in one-sided spikes in early and mid summer and give emphasis to a billowing cloud of mock orange (*Philadelphus coronarius*) whose white flowers have a delicious fragrance of orange blossom.

WHITE AND YELLOW

Yellows and whites make a refreshing partnership, bringing an impression of sunlight to the garden, even on a dull day.

White flowers can benefit from being grown alongside a more positive colour – one that will catch the eye and draw it to the arrangement. Yellow is the perfect partner. While being strong enough to contrast with white, it is not so different that it jars or presents a scene of disunity.

Grown with such strong clear yellows as winter jasmine, forsythia, potentilla, helianthus and rudbeckia, white forms a striking contrast. It seems to deepen the intensity of the yellow, making it clearer, cleaner and more refreshingly distinct.

Pale yellows, on the other hand, harmonize more closely with white creating a gentle, restful design. This can be softened even more with one or two grey foliage plants, which encourage the flower colours to merge, almost losing their individuality, and forming a pleasing misty effect. Pastel yellows and white stand out well at dusk, reflecting every beam of fading evening light, so plant them where they can be seen.

In any association of whites and yellows it pays to have a few flowers which include both colours. These help form a link between the different plants, painting a more unified picture. The Japanese anemone (*Anemone × hybrida*) 'Louise Uhink' is a plant to bear in mind here, with its white petals and conspicuous yellow stamens. Or there's the Shasta daisy (*Chrysanthemum maximum*) with white petals and a central disc of yellow florets. Two bicoloured annuals, ideal for edging a border are tidy tips (*Layia elegans*) and the poached egg flower (*Limnanthes douglasii*).

▲ **White edgings** In mid spring, the tiny flowers of lungwort (*Pulmonaria saccharata* 'White Wings') provide an ideal edging for the yellow daisy flowers of leopard's bane (*Doronicum plantagineum*).

▼ **Pastel shades** In this peaceful summer setting, white is created by the tall spikes of *Veronica virginica* 'Alba' and misty sprays of *Gypsophila paniculata*. Among them grow flat-headed yellow *Achillea* hybrids and, at the front, yellow-green lady's mantle (*Alchemilla mollis*).

◄ **Pearly white** A perfect partnership is created by two members of the daisy family. The large flat, densely bunched heads of yarrow (*Achillea* 'Coronation Gold') stand like golden flames in a sea of simple grey leaves belonging to pearl everlasting (*Anaphalis*). Its white, yellow-tipped flowers match those of yarrow in shape and arrangement and grow in happy association until autumn.

► **Daisy chains** The Shasta daisy (*Chrysanthemum maximum* 'Wirral Pride') makes a stunning central foil for a range of yellow and white shades. Its 90cm (3ft) tall stems bear semi-double white daisy flowers, a shape repeated in the lower-growing, sunny-flowered *Coreopsis verticillata* whose bright green, ferny foliage hides the bare chrysanthemum bases. The white and yellow, late-summer scheme is framed within a background of yellow tree lupins (*Lupinus arboreus*) and a front edging of the white flowers and white-striped leaves of the dead nettle (*Lamium maculatum* 'Album').

WHITE AND PINK

Charming pastel effects can be achieved by grouping soft pinks and reds with white or cream flowers.

▲ **Lime lovers** Dropwort (*Filipendula vulgaris* 'Flore Pleno') creates a creamy froth above the bright pink flowers of *Cistus crispus*.

▼ **Summer pastels** Glowing pink *Geranium endressii* 'Wargrave Pink' stands out against the creamy white foam of goat's beard (*Aruncus*).

Gentle whites and pale pinks create a feeling of spaciousness in a garden. Their simplicity and freshness is appealing during the day and as twilight approaches, they take on a luminescent quality. Although gardens with only white flowers are restful, they can seem monotonous and are improved when blended with at least one other colour chosen to enhance the mood created by white.

Pinks are warmer on the eye and less clinical than white, matching the inherent touch of blue that gives white flowers their crispness. As pinks become richer and more saturated with colour, they appear ever warmer, eventually red and dominant.

Since pinks appear darker against a backcloth of white, the darker the hue, the fewer plants you should use. A large pink patch – particularly if it is light red rather than soft pink – destroys the calm of the white flowers.

When white and pink flowers are combined, the virtues of each are highlighted. Soft pinks seem even gentler when planted with white flowers, which themselves take on a cleaner and still more luminous appearance.

▲ **Pink on pink** Two quite different pinks — the deep carmine of *Filipendula purpurea* in the background and the salmon-pink of *Astilbe* — combine to highlight the slender white flower stems of *Hosta elata*. Its broad, dark green and glossy leaves contrast handsomely with the fine feathery foliage of its partners.

◄ **Silver-white and pink** For late summer and autumn colour, the Michaelmas daisies have few equals. The pure white *Aster novi-belgii* 'Blondie' nestles close to a blue-flowered relation 'Marie Ballard', their daisy flowers providing a foil for the graceful spikes of clear pink Kaffir lily (*Schizostylis coccinea* 'Mrs Hegarty'). A silvery frame of the conifer *Chamaecyparis pisifera* 'Boulevard' at the back and the foliage plant *Santolina chamaecyparissus* at the front holds the composition together.

▲ **Summer meadows** The mound-forming meadow crane's bill (*Geranium pratense* 'Album') blends delightfully with the rose-pink pincushion heads of *Centaurea dealbata*.

▶ **Rose colours** The famous old rambler rose 'Albertine', with a profusion of soft pink, double flowers, marries happily with other old favourites, such as white and pink foxgloves.

▼ **Spring companions** In this eye-catching partnership, tiers of large white flower heads on *Viburnum plicatum* 'Mariesii' cast shade over moisture-loving, pink-magenta Japanese primroses (*Primula japonica*).

◄ **Summer fragrance** The Damask rose 'Mme Hardy' blossoms sumptuously in midsummer with perfectly formed, pure white and green-eyed, scented flowers. At its feet, spicy pink *Geranium endressii* and softer-hued *Dianthus* 'Inchmery', an old-fashioned pink, pay humble homage.

▼ **Close connection** In late spring and early summer, the clustered white heads of the deciduous shrub *Spiraea × vanhouttei* mingle closely with the graceful bleeding heart (*Dicentra spectabilis*). The slender stems are weighed down with symmetrical ranks of heart-shaped, rose-pink bell flowers with protruding and glistening white inner petals.

► **Icy white** In the centre of this outstanding shrub group is the floribunda rose 'Iceberg' that blooms on and off from mid summer to late autumn. In August, it is upstaged by cascades of softest rose-pink tamarisk (*Tamarix pentandra*), a favourite in seaside gardens like its companion, the Spanish broom (*Spartium junceum*) with wand-like stems of bright yellow flowers. The airy group is given substance with a front planting of evergreen, yellow-flowered *Bupleurum fruticosum* and *Hebe* 'Blue Gem'.

▲ White and pink pillars Climbing roses, which do not climb at all but sprawl unless tied to supports, include a group known as pillar roses. They have stiff but supple shoots, less vigorous than other large-flowered climbers, that are wound round and tied to upright supports. As such they achieve spectacular effects, becoming living columns of dramatic dimensions, covered from tip to toe in clusters of bloom.

► Autumn symphony The Japanese anemones (*Anemone × hybrida*) fill the autumn border with cottage-garden charm. Modern hybrids spread to form neat clumps of dark green, vine-like foliage above which rise weaving wands of saucer-shaped blooms with golden-yellow stamens. The pure white 'Honorine Jobert' is an old favourite, mingling with the clear rose-pink of 'Queen Charlotte'.

WHITE AND BLUE

White flowers give depth to all shades of blue, throwing their dusky colours into sharp relief.

Blue flowers evoke sunlit skies and the early days of the growing season when the garden starts to come to life. White gives blue a greater clarity, whether it is the palest blue of *Mertensia virginica* or the intense blue of *Gentiana verna*. The freshness of blue flowers planted with white in woodland is one of the fine delights of spring. For example, drifts of white and clear deep blue *Anemone apennina* in the dappled light beneath deciduous trees are a stunning sight.

One of the best partnerships for a spring bedding scheme is a carpet of forget-me-nots pierced with white tulips. This simple composition provides an intriguing contrast between the small, plain forget-me-not and the tulip's large and elegant goblets.

In early summer, statuesque spikes of blue delphiniums behind double white peonies and the luminous flowers of *Geranium* 'Johnson's Blue' again provide a contrast in flower form. The violet-blue *Geranium × magnificum* is another hardy crane's-bill, whose mounded form and lobed leaves go well with the narrow, upright foliage of white *Iris sibirica*.

Blue flowers are rarer once summer is over, but there is still some choice. In early autumn, 1.8m (6ft) high monkshood (*Aconitum* 'Barker's Variety'), with deep blue hooded flowers, contrasts well with two equally imposing plants: the white bottle brush flowers of bugbane (*Cimicifuga simplex racemosa*) and giant white late-blooming daisies of *Chrysanthemum serotinum*.

▲ **Late-summer partners** The silky blooms of musk mallow (*Malva moschata* 'Alba') glow white behind clouds of lavender-blue sea lavender (*Limonium latifolium*). Easy and undemanding to grow, the flower sprays can be dried for everlasting flowers.

▼ **Woodland spring** Thriving in the moist soil and dappled shade of deciduous trees, these woodland plants make charming companions. The white, three-petalled blooms of wake robin (*Trillium grandiflorum*) contrast in form and colour with the nodding bluebells (*Endymion nonscriptus*).

▶ **Close friends** Sweet alyssum (*Alyssum maritimum*) is a popular edging plant with its dense, fragrant and long-lasting white flowers. It is frequently partnered with another annual, *Lobelia erinus*, available in a range of blue shades — dark blue 'Crystal Palace'; mid blue 'Blue Stone'; and the pale 'Cambridge Blue'.

▼ **Winter in the rock garden** Spring comes early with little nodding snowflakes (*Leucojum vernum*) nestling close to the blue, anemone-like *Hepatica nobilis*. Both need moist soil and shade.

▶ **Summer perfection** Lush clumps of grassy foliage tumble over the waterside edge; in the shimmering sunlight reflected in the smooth surface of a pool, the water iris (*Iris laevigata*) shows off its magnificent blue and white (*I.* 'Alba') blooms.

▼ **White abandon** The fragrant rambler rose 'Sander's White' scrambles among a sea of shining blue and lavender flax (*Linum narbonense*), studded at intervals with the huge, dark purple flower heads of *Allium albopilosum*. On the right, the spiny foliage of bear's breeches (*Acanthus spinosus*) gives strength to the group.

► **Paper white** In late spring, the arching branches of the deciduous, lime-hating shrub *Exochorda racemosa* are festooned with dense clusters of paper-white blooms. Each flower is up to 4cm (1½in) across and opens from globular buds that give the shrub the common name of pearl bush. Its branches reach down to touch the deep blue tubular flowers of lungwort (*Pulmonaria saccharata* 'Highdown'), with its silvery-marked, lance-shaped leaves.

◄ **Year-round pleasure** The semi-evergreen *Cotoneaster* × *watereri* arches its branches to create a pool of shade. In late spring, the white, bell-shaped flowers of Solomon's seal (*Polygonatum* × *hybridum*) hang beneath pale green ribbed leaves. Here, they are followed by drifts of blue bellflowers (*Campanula persicifolia*), outside the shade, flowering at the same time as billowing white clouds on the cotoneaster. Much later, huge clusters of scarlet berries take over which, birds permitting, last well into the winter.

WHITE THROUGH THE YEAR

**White is present in every month, as clumps
of clarity in winter-dreary gardens and as serene
contrasts to summer profusion.**

White flowers predominate in the winter and spring garden when they seem to possess a translucent quality lacking in the ice-cool whites that characterize summer. There can be few sights more welcome than the first snowdrops (*Galanthus nivalis*). They are the first sure sign that spring is on the way, and they are soon joined by pale cream primroses and crocus, hyacinths, narcissi and tulips. Later come the white scented stars of *Magnolia stellata* and the hazy clouds of *Amelanchier canadensis*.

As the sun gets warmer and the light stronger, white flowers become ever crisper and their scent heavier until, in May, the garden is perfumed with top-heavy white lilacs, dainty lilies-of-the-valley and the massed flowers on the mock orange (*Philadelphus* sp.). The ornamental thorn (*Crataegus monogyna*) is smothered with white blossom so heavily scented as to be nearly overpowering.

Then come the pure white open bells of the shrubby *Deutzia × rosea* 'Multiflora', roses and lilies, and the foaming snow-in-summer (*Cerastium biebersteinii*) that threatens to overrun its allotted space. Late summer sees the creamy-white clusters on evergreen *Eucryphia × nymansensis*, the scented spikes on the butterfly bush (*Buddleia davidii* 'White Cloud'), and the tree poppy (*Romneya coulteri*) whose petals look like crushed silk.

In autumn, the white tones become soft again, creamy in the silky plumes of pampas grass (*Cortaderia selloana*) and the evergreen, scented *Osmanthus heterophyllus*, and soft white in the little autumn crocus (*Colchicum speciosum* 'Album'). The winter scene is cheered with white-flowering evergreens like ericas, *Viburnum × burkwoodii*, and the fragrant *Daphne odora* 'Alba'.

▼ **Summer into autumn** Tall lacecap hydrangeas thrive in coastal gardens, displaying their flat flower heads for several months before fading to russet shades.

▶ **Autumn mists** A cloud of tiny, double white flowers of the perennial baby's breath (*Gypsophila paniculata* 'Bristol Fairy') creates a misty background for the daisy-like, bronze-red flowers of *Helenium autumnale* 'Moerheim Beauty'. Both are long-lasting as cut flowers.

▲ **Shades of autumn** The creamy feathery plumes of pampas grass (*Cortaderia selloana*) steal the scene in this impressive autumn planting — but not completely. On the left, the variegated foliage of a bold clump of zebra grass (*Miscanthus sinensis* 'Zebrinus') adds another autumnal touch. In front, the slender stems of the half-hardy fountain grass (*Pennisetum setaceum*), set with silky cream spikelets, add another variation on an all-grass theme.

◀ **Winter joy** The common snowdrop, known more poetically as 'Fair Maids of February', is not always easy to establish. It thrives in cool soil and in the shade of deciduous trees and shows its resentment at any upheaval by taking its time to settle down again. But once it is contented, it will push the familiar white bells above ground whatever the winter weather and spread to form carpeting colonies.

▲ **Frosty white** One variety of the spring-flowering Fuji cherry, *Prunus incisa* 'Praecox', blooms in late winter, studding its naked branches with pure white flowers that open from pale pink buds. The small, toothed leaves are splendidly coloured in autumn. The variety is much used for dwarfed bonsai trees.

◄ **Christmas blooms** The opening buds of *Helleborus niger* can be encouraged into bloom for Christmas Day by covering the evergreen clumps with cloches to protect them from the weather. The common name of Christmas rose reflects the time of flowering and the shape of the blooms. Shiny white and satiny in texture, the petals are sometimes stained rose-purple at the base and surround a centre of golden anthers.

▲ **Spring harbingers** The pure white and clear blue flowers of the little wood anemone (*Anemone apennina*), held on slender stems above ferny foliage, dominate a spring border carpeted with sky-blue *Scilla sibirica*. The pastel shades soften the rich maroon cups of the Lenten rose (*Helleborus orientalis*).

▶ **April showers** The spectacular blossoms of a flowering cherry tree will soon shed their white petals over a naturalized planting of cream and golden narcissi trumpets mingled with cottage tulips in red and yellow. Together, they create the epitome of an English spring garden.

▲ **May blossom** The sweetly scented garden lilacs are cultivars of *Syringa vulgaris* specially bred for the purity of flower colours which range from white, cream and yellow through all the shades of pink, red, blue and purple. The dense, pure white panicles contrast effectively in form and colour with the neighbouring rose-pink rhododendron.

◄ **Summer snow** In spite of its name, the summer snowflake (*Leucojum aestivum*), with sprays of nodding bell-like flowers, blooms in April and May, at the same time as the orange-gold tulip 'General de Wet'. The snowflake's narrow leaves contrast well with the broader, lighter green tulip foliage.

73

▲ Spring skies The pure white flowers of the fragrant *Daphne mezereum* 'Alba' above the intense blue bells of *Scilla sibirica* 'Spring Beauty' reflect scudding clouds on a blue March sky.

► Rose arbours In early summer, a scented pergola of white, pink and red roses underplanted with silvery-grey foliage plants holds all the promise of long sunny days.

▼ Summer perfection In this early summer scene, an edging of nicotianas is balanced by an urn of *Chrysanthemum frutescens*, while the shape of spectacular rhododendrons is repeated in a backdrop of *Viburnum × carlcephalum*.

WHITE AND CREAM-COLOURED FLOWERS

	NAME	DESCRIPTION	HEIGHT	SEASON
TREES	*Arbutus unedo*	Evergreen glossy foliage; loamy soil; sun	4.5m (15ft)	Autumn
	Catalpa bignonioides	Deciduous; long seed pods. Any soil; sun	6m (20ft)	Summer
	Halesia carolina, H. monticola	Deciduous; moist, lime-free soil; shelter	7.5m (25ft)	Spring
	Malus hupehensis, M. x robusta	Deciduous; autumn fruit; any soil; sun	4.5m (15ft)	Spring
	Sophora japonica 'Regent'	Deciduous; good soil; sun and shelter	7.5m (25ft)	Late summer
	Sorbus species and vars.	Deciduous; autumn tints/berries; any soil; sun	4.5-6m (15-20ft)	Spring
	Stewartia species	Deciduous; autumn tints, good bark; acid soil	3.5-6m (12-20ft)	Summer
	Styrax japonica	Deciduous; moist acid soil; sun and shelter	6m (20ft)	Summer
SHRUBS	*Abelia x grandiflora*	Semi-evergreen; any soil; sun and shelter	0.9-1.2m (3-4ft)	Summer-autumn
	Abutilon vitifolium 'Tennant's White'	Evergreen; any soil, sunny wall	2.4m (8ft)	Spring-autumn
	Carpenteria californica	Evergreen; good soil; full sun	3m (10ft)	Summer
	Choisya ternata	Evergreen; good soil; sun and shelter	1.5m (5ft)	Late spring
	Clematis species and vars.	Hardy deciduous climbers; neutral soil; sun	1.8-12m (6-40ft)	Spring-autumn
	Clethra alnifolia	Deciduous; rich moist, acid soil; sun/shade	1.8-2.4m (6-8ft)	Summer-autumn
	Cornus florida, C. nuttallii	Deciduous; moist soil; sun or light shade	3-7.5m (10-25ft)	Late spring
	Cytisus x kewensis	Deciduous, spreading; any, poor soil; full sun	30-60cm (1-2ft)	Late spring
	Hebe albicans; H. 'Pagei'	Evergreen; ordinary soil; full sun/shelter	15-60cm (6-24in)	Summer
	Helianthemum nummularium vars.	Evergreen; well-drained soil; full sun	10-15cm (4-6in)	Summer
	Hoheria lyallii	Deciduous; half-hardy; any soil; sun/shelter	3-4.5m (10-15ft)	Summer
	Hydrangea arborescens 'Grandiflora'	Deciduous; moist loam; sun or light shade	1.2-1.8m (4-6ft)	Summer-autumn
	Jasminum officinale	Deciduous climber; well-drained soil; shelter	9m (30ft)	Summer-autumn
	Leucothoë fontanesiana	Semi-evergreen; moist acid soil; shade	1.2m (4ft)	Late spring
	Lonicera fragrantissima, L. standishii	Semi-evergreen, scented; well-drained soil; sun	1.2-1.8m (4-6ft)	Winter-spring
	Magnolia species and vars.	Deciduous; well-drained loam; shelter	1.8-10m (6-33ft)	Spring, summer
	Osmanthus x burkwoodii	Evergreen; well-drained soil; sun/shelter	1.8-3m (6-10ft)	Spring
	Pieris species and vars.	Evergreen, young leaves red; acid soil, shelter	1.2-3m (4-10ft)	Spring
	Polygonum baldschuanicum	Deciduous strong climber; any soil; sun or shade	12m (40ft)	Summer-autumn
	Prunus species, numerous vars.	Deciduous; good autumn tints, bark; any soil; sun	0.6-6m (2-20ft)	Winter-late spring
	Ribes sanguineum 'Album'	Deciduous; scented; well-drained soil; sun	1.8m (6ft)	Late spring
	Rubus x tridel 'Benenden'	Deciduous, fast-growing; any soil; sun	1.8-2.4m (6-7ft)	Late spring-summer
	Skimmia japonica, S. reevesiana	Evergreen; berries; any soil, sun or shade	0.9-1.5m (3-5ft)	Spring
	Solanum jasminoides 'Album'	Evergreen cliumber; ordinary soil; warm wall	3-4.5m (10-15ft)	Summer-autumn
	Sorbaria aitchisonii	Deciduous, ferny leaves; any soil, sun or shade	1.8-2.7m (6-9ft)	Late summer-autumn
	Trachelospermum jasminoides	Evergreen climber; fragrant; acid soil; warm wall	3-3.6m (10-12ft)	Summer
	Vinca minor 'Alba'	Evergreen ground cover; any soil; shade	5-10cm (2-4in)	Spring-autumn
	Weigela 'Mont Blanc'	Deciduous; well-drained soil; sun/light shade	1.5-1.8m (5-6ft)	Early summer
	Wisteria sinensis 'Alba'	Deciduous climber; deep soil; sunny wall	21m (70ft)	Spring-summer

BORDER PLANTS

NAME	DESCRIPTION/SITE	HEIGHT	SEASON
Achillea ptarmica 'The Pearl'	Wide-spreading; well-drained soil; sun	75cm (2½ft)	Late summer
Anaphalis species	Silvery leaves; well-drained soil; sun	30-60cm (1-2ft)	Summer-autumn
Androsace carnea	Evergreen rock plant; well-drained soil; sun	2.5-10cm (1-4in)	Early summer
Anthemis cupaniana	Grey foliage; any soil; sun	30cm (1ft)	All summer
Arabis caucasica	Evergreen rock plant; well-drained soil; shade	10-23cm (4-9in)	Late winter-summer
Arenaria balearica, A. montana	Evergreen rock plants; gritty soil; shade	2.5-15cm (1-6in)	Spring-summer
Astilbe species and vars.	Handsome foliage; moist soil; sun/light shade	45cm-1.2m (1½-4ft)	Summer
Camassia leichtlinii	Bulbous; rich moist soil; sun or light shade	90cm (3ft)	Summer
Celmisia species	Silvery felted leaves; rich soil; sun/shelter	2.5-23cm (1-9in)	Spring-summer
Cimicifuga species	Handsome foliage; moist rich soil; light shade	0.6-1.8m (2-6ft)	Summer-autumn
Clematis recta	Border plant, scented; ordinary soil; sun	1.2m (4ft)	Summer
Convallaria majalis	Fragrant lily-of-the-valley; moist soil; shade	15-20cm (6-8in)	Late spring
Crambe cordifolia	Huge heart-shaped leaves; rich soil; sun	1.8m (6ft)	Summer
Dictamnus albus	Lemon-scented; volatile oils; any soil; sun	0.6-1m (2-3ft)	Summer
Dryas octopetala	Evergreen rock plant; well-drained soil; sun	7.5-10cm (3-4in)	Summer
Filipendula ulmaria	Large palmate leaves; moist soil; sun	90cm (3ft)	Summer
Galium odoratum	Ground-cover plant; moist soil; sun or shade	25cm (10in)	Spring-summer
Galtonia candicans	Bulbous; any soil; full sun	1.2m (4ft)	Summer-autumn
Hutchinsia alpina	Evergreen rock plant; well-drained cool soil	7.5-10cm (3-4in)	Summer
Iberis sempervirens	Evergreen, spreading; any soil; sun	23cm (9in)	Spring-summer
Ipheion uniflorum	Bulbous, scented; any soil; sun/shelter	10-15cm (4-6in)	Spring
Leontopodium alpinum	Rock plant; gritty soil; full sun	15cm (6in)	Summer
Liatris scariosa 'Snow White'	Grassy clumps; moist soil; full sun	1.8m (6ft)	Summer-autumn
Lysimachia clethroides	Wide-spreading; moist soil; sun or shade	90cm (3ft)	Summer-autumn
Macleaya cordata	Large lobed leaves; good loam; sun/shelter	2.4m (8ft)	All summer
Nierembergia repens	Carpeting plant; well-drained soil; sun	5cm (2in)	All summer
Ornithogalum umbellatum	Bulb for naturalizing; well-drained soil; sun	15cm (6in)	Spring
Oxalis enneaphylla	Carpeting plant; rich soil; sun	7.5cm (3in)	Summer
Polygonatum species	Arching stems; moist acid soil; shade	0.6-1.8m (2-6ft)	Spring-summer
Primula reidii	Hairy leaves; bell flowers; moist soil; sun	10cm (4in)	Late spring
Raoulia glabra	Carpeting evergreen; any soil; sun	Prostrate	Spring
Rodgersia species	Foliage plants; moist soil, light shade	0.9-1.8m (3-6ft)	Summer
Sanguinaria canadensis	Rock plant; rich well-drained soil; sun	15-20cm (6-8in)	Spring
Saxifraga species and vars.	Evergreen rosettes; well-drained soil; sun	2.5-45cm (1-18in)	Late winter-autumn
Silene alpestris, S. maritima	Evergreen; any soil; sun or light shade	15-20cm (6-8in)	Summer-autumn
Sisyrinchium striatum	Evergreen, grassy; rich soil; sun	45cm (1½ft)	Summer
Smilacina racemosa	Arching stems; rich moist soil; shade	90cm (3ft)	Spring-summer
Symphytum grandiflorum	Ground-cover plant; any soil; sun/shade	20cm (8in)	Spring-summer
Tiarella cordifolia	Semi-evergreen; moist soil; cool shade	30cm (1ft)	Spring-summer
Veratrum album	Handsome leaves; moist soil; light shade	1.2m (4ft)	Summer

Yellow and orange flowers

Yellow is a cheerful, sunny colour, which is often particularly associated with spring flowers such as aconites, narcissi, primulas and forsythia. However, it is also found in summer and autumn gardens, as well as in the bright winter splashes of mahonias, winter jasmines and witch hazels. Being so close to green in the colour spectrum, yellow harmonizes well with most foliage, notably soft green and grey; and yellow foliage itself should never be overlooked.

After white, yellow is the most eye-catching colour in the garden. It is luminous and stands out distinctly at a distance, thus appearing to be closer than it really is. Perceived as a warm colour, yellow varies in shade from palest pastel yellow to clear primrose, dusty sulphur to bright gold, and orange-red to peach and apricot, with many shades and combinations of muted colours between.

All shades of yellow are ideal for creating single-colour schemes in the garden, especially in lightly shaded areas. For maximum effect, plant yellow flowers in bold drifts and clumps rather than dotting them about in small patches. Some yellow tones, such as apricot and pale yellow-orange, can lose their intensity next to clear yellow shades, and look their best in foliage settings.

The *Compositae* (daisy) family includes a vast range of yellow and orange flowers; other sources of yellow are numerous, and include spring bulbs, many roses, dahlias and chrysanthemums, and irises and yarrows. It is also worth seeking out lesser-known yellow-flowered plants such as *Delphinium* 'Butterball', the pale yellow *Nicotiana* strain, *Rhododendron luteum*, the gold-leaved Mexican orange *Choisya ternata* 'Sundance', and *Clematis tangutica* with its lantern-like rich yellow flowers in late summer and autumn.

Gold and yellow Orange-gold honeysuckle arches over golden marjoram and Welsh poppies.

SHADES OF YELLOW

Use yellow flowers and golden foliage to create focal points in the garden or bring sunny hues to dark, shaded corners.

When introducing single colour planting schemes to a garden, it's essential to consider the qualities of that colour. This should help you to come up with an effective site for the planting – half the story of successful plant design.

Yellow is perceived by our eyes more quickly than any other colour – it immediately attracts attention. So all-yellow plantings are ideal for drawing attention to a particular feature in the garden or for forming focal points.

Yellow flowers are also luminous – a quality which makes them perfect for cheering up dark shady corners, creating deceptive vistas and for filling containers and beds around a patio used in the fading evening light.

In any all-yellow planting try to introduce different hues – not a difficult task when you consider the enormous range available – from soft cream through primrose, lemon, green-yellow and butter to rich gold and orange of a dazzling intensity. Such contrasting shades will make the picture more interesting and also create a sense of depth. When pale yellow flowers such as verbascum grow alongside the warmer, more intense yellow of *Achillea*, for example, the former tend to recede, giving the grouping depth.

Another trick for making your yellow planting stimulating to the eye is to combine species whose flower shapes and textures differ. A mass planting of clear yellow, goblet-shaped tulips with their satiny petals and packed clusters of golden wallflowers, all edged with sprays of *Alyssum saxatile*, makes a most effective spring planting for an island bed.

To prevent associations of yellow-flowered plants from being too startling, set them off with a foil of fresh green foliage. You'll find this provides for a more restful scene without detracting from the excitement.

Yellow flowers are not the only way of introducing pools of sunlight to beds and borders. Golden-leaved or yellow-leaved plants can be just as successful, either interspersed with green foliage or used to echo yellow-flowered species. They have the advantage of a longer-lasting display than most flowers. Indeed such evergreens as variegated holly and ivy, euonymus, golden privet, and elaeagnus will ensure a splash of colour all through the year, even in the depths of winter.

▼ **Yellow daisies** In high summer, a corner of a herbaceous border is bright with sunshine-yellow daisies backed by pale loosestrife (*Lysimachia punctata*) and golden, double-flowered sunflowers (*Helianthus decapetalus*).

◄ **Yellow brooms** In May, the Warminster broom (*Cytisus × praecox*) cascades sprays of creamy-yellow blossom to continue the yellow theme beneath the developing leaves and fading flowers of *Forsythia suspensa* and *Ribes sanguineum* 'Album'.

▲ **Chrome-yellow and green** The flower-like bracts of the evergreen, shrubby *Euphorbia polychroma* shine like bright yellow suns on late-spring days and reflect the sheen on the dwarf *Chamaecyparis* 'Golden Mop'.

◄ **Form and colour contrasts** In this simple but fascinating partnership of gold and yellow, the contrasting shapes of red-hot poker (*Kniphofia* hybrids) and the flat heads of *Achillea filipendulina* 'Gold Plate' form an impressive combination.

▼ **Waterside plants** Bright yellow spikes of *Lysimachia punctata* challenge the foamy, yellow-green blooms of *Alchemilla mollis* whose soft green leaves contrast with the sword-shaped foliage of water iris.

◄ **Gold foliage** The cut-leaved golden elder (*Sambucus racemosa* 'Plumosa Aurea') has finely dissected, golden-yellow foliage that opens pink-tinted in spring, before the upright clusters of creamy-white flowers. The leaves retain their colour throughout the growing season, especially in light shade, and contrast with the scarlet berries in late summer. A ground cover of golden lemon balm (*Melissa officinalis* 'Aurea') reinforces the scheme.

▼ **Bewitching in winter** The witch hazels are popular shrubs for the winter garden, none more so than *Hamamelis mollis* 'Pallida' whose naked branches are crowded with scented, sulphur-yellow flowers. Here it is underplanted with variegated *Euonymus japonicus* 'Duc d'Anjou' and bright Christmas box (*Sarcococca confusa*).

YELLOW AND GREEN

**Bring out the radiance of yellow and
golden flowers by setting them in the company of
green and yellow foliage.**

Green, in its many tints and shades, is the perfect background for other colours. When combined with yellow – a component of green, together with blue – the result is one of harmony. Yellow and gold are found not only in flowers but also in the variegated and all-yellow foliage of trees, shrubs, grasses and perennial plants.

The long lime-green catkins of the evergreen shrub *Garrya*

elliptica are highly decorative from early autumn to late spring. Alongside, the yellow blooms and bare, greenish stems of winter-flowering jasmine (*Jasminum nudiflorum*) make a delightful partner. Both could be under-planted with late-winter blooming *Crocus aureus* and *Narcissus* 'February Gold'.

Several spurges have blends of green and yellow foliage and

flower bracts, one of the best being *Euphorbia polychroma*, whose yellow bracts are borne in mid and late spring on a 45cm (1½ft) high hummock. The fresh yellow leaves of Bowles' golden grass (*Milium effusum* 'Aureum') make an ideal colour match and provide variety with their contrasting shape. A clump of Viridiflora tulips, such as 'Golden Artist' which has golden yellow flowers and green splashes on fringed petals, could add the finishing touch.

For an evergreen, late-spring combination in shade start with the spurge, *Euphorbia robbiae*. It has yellow-green bracts and narrow dark green leaves that could contrast with the pale green, scalloped foliage of *Tellima grandiflora* 'Purpurea'. Also green-flowered, its foliage turns purple in the autumn. Plant the primrose-yellow speckled leaves of *Tolmiea menziesii* 'Variegata' to bring brightness to the scene.

During the summer *Sisyrinchium striatum*, with erect iris-like pale green leaves some 30cm (1ft) high, has creamy yellow flowers on spikes that rise as much again. For foliage contrast, try *Santolina virens*, with its rich green, finely divided leaves and bright yellow flowers in mid summer. Complete the group by planting in front the golden yellow star-like flowers and green serrated leaves of lime-hating *Chrysogonum virginianum*.

Too much yellow or green could become dull; to prevent monotony, choose different shaped flowers in varying tones of the same colour. In late summer and early autumn the golden yellow daisies of *Helenium autumnale* look eye-catching if backed by the scented, yellowish green flower plumes and jagged green leaves of mugwort (*Artemisia lactiflora*).

◄ **Gold and green foliage** The ribbon-like foliage of the golden-variegated grass *Hakonechloa macra* 'Aureola' contrasts handsomely with the broad, glossy green and deeply veined leaves of *Hosta sieboldiana*.

▲ **Yellow poppies** Yellow or orange Welsh poppies (*Meconopsis cambrica*) take on a luminous quality against a background of the variegated dogwood (*Cornus alba* 'Elegantissima'). Welsh poppies, which are short-lived but seed themselves freely, flower throughout the summer and well into autumn.

◄ **Winter sunshine** The evergreen, glossy-leaved *Mahonia japonica* is one of the pearls in the winter garden. Its lemon-yellow, fragrant flower sprays are borne throughout winter to be joined in early spring by the lime-green flower clusters of Corsican hellebore (*Helleborus lividus corsicus*) rising above an underplanting of snowdrops, pale blue *Iris reticulata* and the creeping ivy (*Hedera helix* 'Glacier').

◄ **Double harmony** Statuesque pale yellow, double-flowered hollyhocks (*Althaea*) are contrasted with the 1.8m (6ft) tall, weaving stems of the graceful grass *Stipa gigantea*. The perennial sunflower (*Helianthus decapetalus* 'Loddon Gold') repeats the double-flowered theme with golden blooms at the lower level. In the foreground, the golden privet (*Ligustrum ovalifolium* 'Aureum') reiterates the yellow and green statement with its variegated leaves.

▼ **Primrose yellow** In late spring, *Rhododendron* 'Goldsworth Yellow' opens its magnificent trusses from apricot-pink buds to pale primrose-yellow blooms. It towers above the elegant stems of Solomon's seal (*Polygonatum* × *hybridum*) hung with white bells above a colour coordinated front planting of white-edged *Hosta crispula*. By autumn, the hosta foliage will turn soft yellow.

▲ **Sulphur-yellow** The miniature *Gladiolus* 'Greenbird' bears spikes of up to ten softly frilled florets of clearest sulphur-yellow suffused with green.

▼ **Yellow fringes** The fringecup (*Tellima grandiflora*) provides an evergreen ground cover of bright green, maple-like leaves. In late spring and summer, slender spikes of bell-shaped flowers stand like streaks of pale yellow above the green foliage.

▲ **Shady companions** The perennial spurges are wonderful elements in the garden scene, with their architectural form, attractive foliage and long-lasting bracts. The semi-evergreen *Euphorbia characias* forms clumps 90cm (3ft) high and wide, of narrow blue-green leaves topped in late spring and early summer with huge heads of brown-eyed, lime-green inflorescences that gradually change to sulphur-yellow. In spite of its Mediterranean origin, this spurge does not object to light shade and is useful for brightening dull corners — here it is in association with a gold-variegated ivy (*Hedera*).

YELLOW AND ORANGE

Mix pale yellow with bright orange in fascinating and complementary schemes offset with fresh green foliage.

Yellow and orange have a lot to be said for them. They're bright – something few gardeners can resist – they clamour for attention, and many attractive species come in these hues.

Planted separately, though, yellow and orange have their drawbacks. Pale yellow can look rather cool and even white at twilight, and often appears to be drained of colour in bright sun. Orange, on the other hand, is warm but lacks the luminosity of yellow, failing to stand out in poor light. If you plant the two together, however, each colour seems to make up for the other's shortcomings, creating perfect partnerships. Mid-green foliage

provides the best background for creating truly harmonious pictures using these sunny colours.

Such associations can be created from totally different plants, but it is often much more satisfactory to create schemes centred round a particular species. Thanks to plant breeders, many species now come in both yellow and orange varieties. If you're considering annual bedding schemes there are pot and French marigolds, nasturtiums, wallflowers and gazanias. When it comes to perennials there are euphorbias, montbretias and heleniums, while the choice of shrubs includes potentillas, pyracanthas, azaleas, berberis, rock roses and helianthemums.

▲ **Perfect partners** In light shade, orange Welsh poppies (*Meconopsis cambrica* 'Aurantiaca') nestle happily beneath 90cm (3ft) tall spikes of an unusual creamy-yellow foxglove (*Digitalis grandiflora*) which flowers from mid to late summer.

▼ **Sunny colours** An eye-catching picture is created simply by planting mixed orange and yellow nasturtiums (*Tropaeolum majus* 'Alaska Mixed'). They scramble and clamber in full sun and poor soil, blaring their trumpets over marbled leaves.

▲ **Autumn glow** The evergreen firethorns are among our most accommodating garden shrubs. In summer they are wreathed in great airy clusters of creamy-white hawthorn-like flowers — though without that delicious scent — and in autumn they are festooned with long-lasting, brilliantly coloured berries as in *Pyracantha coccinea* 'Orange Glow' and 'Golden Charm'. They will grow in any soil and against walls of any aspect.

◄ **Summer exotics** In the shelter of a wall, the orange-red blooms of purple-leaved *Canna* × *generalis* 'Wyoming' glow dramatically in late summer sun. They are contrasted, in form and hues, with dainty apricot-yellow flowers of montbretia (*Crocosmia crocosmiiflora* 'Solfatare') in front. A deep yellow bedding dahlia bridges these two extremes of the yellow colour range.

◄ Summer annuals Yellow and orange-coloured annuals create a profusion of dazzlingly sunny colours during the height of summer. Tall graceful cosmos, with feathery leaves, tower at the back in a range of yellow and orange shades from the mixture *Cosmos sulphureus* 'Bright Lights'. At the front is a bushy edging of the low-growing *Tagetes tenuifolia*, one of the many marigolds in a range of yellow and orange.

Such sunny combinations need the relief of fresh green foliage. Here, this is provided by annual summer cypresses (*Kochia scoparia*) whose symmetrical mounds of light green leaves turn red in autumn.

► Spring carpets A bed of polyanthus primulas in pale yellow, apricot and orange (the 'Barnhaven' strain) is edged with an unusual biscuit-coloured variety of *Alyssum saxatile*, 'Dudley Neville'. The tulips at the back of the bed are tall Darwin hybrids 'Beauty of Apeldoorn', with creamy-yellow petals overlaid with orange; their lovely colours are perfectly matched by the shorter 'General de Wet' tulips, golden-orange and stippled with scarlet.

◄ **Golden rods** In late summer and early autumn, the yellow flowers of *Solidago* weave fluffy clusters at the back of many borders. Their airy form is given substance and their pale colour depth by clumps of sneezeweed (*Helenium autumnale*). The daisy-like flowers of the sneezeweed have prominent, colour-contrasting centres, and are available in a range of colours that includes shades of yellow and orange, from purest sun-yellow to deepest mahogany-orange and fiery reds.

► **Orange and yellow**
In late spring two euphorbias make the ideal marriage: the taller *Euphorbia griffithii* 'Fireglow' flaunts fiery orange bracts next to demure, bright yellow *Euphorbia polychroma*. The small poached egg flower (*Limnanthes douglasii*), with its scented primrose-like flowers of deep yellow edged with white, stands in attendance. Although an annual, it self-seeds to appear year after year.

YELLOW AND BLUE

**Yellow and blue is always successful
– the contrast between warm yellow and
cooler blue is eye-catching.**

Most people probably think of blue and yellow as a spring partnership. A low carpet of primroses with grape hyacinths or scillas forms a very happy combination in early spring – especially under deciduous trees before they come into leaf. And taller combinations of daffodils and bluebells are equally attractive.

The beauty of this colour combination, though, is that it is just as successful in summer – and autumn as well. When such flowers as petunias, salvias, peonies and roses are flaunting their brilliant, hot shades of red and purple, the yellows and blues seem refreshing and cooling. Golden achilleas, doronicums or solidago and blue delphiniums, campanulas and lobelias are just a few of the many successful schemes.

In autumn, an association of misty blue caryopteris with yellow dahlias is most effective, and even in late winter there's a delightful blue/yellow combination – yellow winter aconites interspersed with clumps of deep blue *Iris reticulata*.

Plan your planting with an eye to the height, spread and flowering time of each species.

▲ **Summer annuals** Bright yellow and white poached egg flowers (*Limnanthes douglasii*) mix with baby blue-eyes (*Nemophila menziesii*) in a cheerful, low border edging.

▼ **Yellow foam** Yellow-green sprays of lady's mantle (*Alchemilla mollis*) tumble among cool summer blues, such as perennial veronicas, lobelias, larkspurs, linums and polemoniums.

◄ **Late-summer sheen** At the back of a border, the rich golden daisy flowers of the 1.2m (4ft) tall coneflower (*Rudbeckia*) contrast perfectly in colour and form with the metallic-blue, spiny heads of the globe thistle (*Echinops ritro*). The globe thistle is an excellent choice for cutting and drying for winter decoration.

▲ **Spring carpets** Bright sun in late spring brings out the clear colours of yellow, lily-flowered tulips rising above a carpet of blue forget-me-nots. These little biennials seed themselves freely — and in places where they are not wanted; they can be thinned out ruthlessly as flowering finishes.

► **Creeping yellows** In high summer, the shrubby St John's wort (*Hypericum olympicum*) trails its golden flowers over the rock garden, close to the sprawling stems of bright blue speedwell (*Veronica prostrata*). On the left, a clump of yellow flax (*Linum flavum*) is more restrained.

YELLOW AND MAUVE

Putting mauve and yellow together makes for a daring colour partnership that requires careful choice of plants. When successful, the match creates stunning effects.

When mauve flowers are blended with other similarly coloured blooms, the effect is muted. Add yellow flowers or foliage, and the scene becomes livelier. However there is a catch; where both colours are brilliant – deep purple and rich yellow, for instance – the association will jar rather than entice. Always match bright yellows with subdued mauves or soft, subtle yellows with bright mauves.

In early and mid spring the bare branches of forsythia are thickly covered with yellow bell-like flowers. Cool this brilliance by underplanting with drifts of large-flowered mauve crocuses: 'Pickwick', for example, has pale lilac petals feathered with stripes of a deeper colour.

At the same time of the year, clumps of creamy yellow common primrose (*Primula vulgaris*) mingle well with the mauvish petals of dog's-tooth violet (*Erythronium dens-canis*) – a combination readily found in the wild. As both plants are low growing, add height by introducing drifts of the 30cm (1ft) tall wild daffodil (*Narcissus pseudonarcissus*).

Erysimum 'Bowles' Mauve' is a sub-shrubby perennial wallflower with rosettes of grey-green leaves topped by lilac-mauve flowers from early summer onwards. It needs a well-drained sunny site and makes an excellent partner for the low-growing golden sage (*Salvia officinalis* 'Icterina') whose leaves are marked with primrose and gold.

Another sun-loving shrub is the 1.2m (4ft) evergreen Jerusalem sage (*Phlomis fruticosa*). With hairy, grey-green wrinkled leaves, it has whorls of hooded yellow flowers that appear during the summer. For contrast in flower colour and shape, use it as a background for *Hebe* 'Bowles' Hybrid'. This is about half the height of the Jerusalem sage and has narrow, pale green glossy leaves, with mauve flowers during summer and autumn,. The hebe also looks good with the equally long-flowering *Potentilla fruticosa* 'Goldfinger' – a twiggy compact shrub of the same height as the hebe, but with deep yellow flowers and small divided leaves.

Several hostas have flowers in pale lilacs and mauves. The aptly named 'Tall Boy' has fresh green, heart-shaped leaves with flowering stems up to 1.2m (4ft) high. The lobed leaves of the flowering currant (*Ribes sanguineum*), in its yellow-leaved form 'Brocklebankii', would make a complementary backcloth for the hosta's violet-mauve flowers.

Michaelmas daisies (*Aster novi-belgii*) come into their own in early autumn. There are several varieties with mauve-blue flowers, such as the 90cm (3ft) tall, double-flowered 'Ada Ballard'. The dahlia 'Deepest Yellow', with richly coloured flowerheads in the form of neat, tight balls, makes a pleasant companion.

◀ **Climbing duet** In early and mid summer, the golden-yellow flowers of the climbing variety of the semi-double rose 'Allgold' contrast delightfully with the deep lavender-mauve flowers of *Clematis* 'Lasurstern'.

▲ Evening primrose At the front of a border, the evening primrose (*Oenothera missouriensis*) opens its satiny, pale yellow flowers during the day as well as at dusk. It blooms throughout summer, in happy association with the much taller, glossy-leaved *Eryngium variifolium* whose evergreen foliage is marked with silvery veins that match the bracts around its mauve-blue flower globes.

◄ Yellow yarrows The large, flat-topped heads of yarrows (*Achillea*) are popular subjects for the herbaceous border. They give substance to more fleeting flowers and bloom without any fuss throughout summer and early autumn. *Achillea filipendulina* 'Gold Plate', at a height of 1.2m (4ft), is best sited at the back of a border where its deep yellow flower heads can contrast with the fragrant, mauve-purple clusters of *Verbena bonariensis*. Although this is not reliably hardy, it seeds itself freely and seedlings appear each spring.

◄ Sunny spring The lovely bulbous *Iris bucharia* creates stunning focal points in large rock gardens during late spring. Carrying up to six flowers on each of its 45cm (1½ft) tall stems, rising between glossy grey-green leaves, the bright yellow and creamy-white blooms create patches of sunshine on the dullest day, especially when viewed against a dark background. A clump of the elegant little pasque flower (*Pulsatilla vulgaris*) provides contrast in shape, colour and foliage, with large goblet-shaped, downy and mauve blooms nodding above ferny leaves.

◀ **Golden rain** The brilliant yellow, pendent trusses, as much as 60cm (2ft) long, of *Laburnum × watereri* 'Vossii' soften the intensity of a purple-violet underplanting. The ornamental onions are spectacular border plants, but the fiery colour of the large flower globes on *Allium rosenbachianum* requires careful handling in an early-summer border with softer-toned inhabitants.

▼ **Gentle summer tints** A harmonious blend of soft colours creates a restful yet highly pleasing border of pale yellows and lavender-blues. Silvery-mauve pansies at the front complement the giant bellflower (*Campanula latifolia*) whose purple-blue bells borrow warmth from fluffy, pale yellow and dwarf golden rods (*Solidago* 'Lemore'). The golden daisies of *Inula hookeri* and tall-stemmed hollyhocks of palest primrose-yellow paint still more delicate shades.

▲ **Dressed down** The clear yellow and orange of Welsh poppies (*Meconopsis cambrica*) lighten the deep magenta of black-eyed *Geranium psilostemon* flowering during the summer.

▲ Cascades of mauve Trained along wire supports, the large purple-blue flowers of late-summer flowering *Clematis* 'The President' tumble among the branches of a dogwood (*Cornus alba* 'Spaethii'). Its golden variegated leaves add lustre to the sea of purple, reinforced by a low-growing shrubby cinquefoil (*Potentilla fruticosa*) with delicate primrose-yellow blooms.

▲ Winter willows The thick black buds that stud the Japanese willow (*Salix gracilistyla* 'Melanostachys') through the winter months shed their shells in February to reveal velvety, crimson-jet catkins. By March these burst into showers of golden pollen. Only one thing — golden trumpet daffodils — can match the splendour.

◄ Gold dust Flowering profusely from early spring and into summer, mat-forming, purple aubrietas are easy to grow in sunny rock gardens and on banks and walls. Their trusted companion is the easy-going *Alyssum montanum* 'Mountain Gold' whose clusters of tiny golden stars bob through the sea of purple.

YELLOW THROUGH THE YEAR

**Yellow shades match the sun, from pale
lemon in winter to gold in spring and summer,
and the fiery orange of an autumn sunset.**

During the bleakest months of the year, yellow flowers bring the promise of spring. The dullest day is brightened at the sight of a winter jasmine against a wall or a small clump of aconites lifting yellow faces above fallen winter-brown leaves. Early narcissi – the shy little trumpets of 'Peeping Tom' or the hoop petticoats of *Narcissus bulbocodium* – are fore runners of the yellow, golden and orange sheets to come from spring daffodils and crocus, from tulips and irises, and from bright yellow forsythia and the golden butter-cups of *Kerria japonica*.

Yellow turns to gold with the flowering brooms and barberries, with primroses and cowslips, eri-gerons and globe flowers (*Trollius europaeus*). Late spring is the season for the magnificent rhododendrons and azaleas, like the creamy-yellow *Rhododendron* 'Queen Elizabeth II' and the gloriously massed gold of 'Narcissiflorum' azaleas. Summer is heralded by early roses – dainty, bright-faced 'Canary Bird' and the heady-scented pale golden blooms of 'Frühlingsgold.' There are golden laburnums and lilacs (*Syringa* 'Primrose') at one level, with potentillas and hypericums on the ground floor. Borders can be filled with tall ligularias and pale yellow verbascums, peonies and yarrows (*Achillea* species) in shades of sulphur or deep gold.

Autumn comes with rudbeckias and heleniums, dahlias and chrysanthemums, with tall, double-flowered helianthus and the creamy-yellow funnels of *Kirengeshoma palmata*. There are edgings of marigolds and self-sown drifts of Californian poppies (*Eschscholzia californica*), gold and orange leaf tints and clusters of fruit and berries on crab apples, whitebeams and firethorns.

▼ **Late-summer sun** Clear yellow montbretias (*Crocosmia* 'Citronella') form the centrepiece in this late-summer scene. Their dark green, strap-shaped leaves are echoed and contrasted in a tall clump of green and yellow variegated New Zealand flax (*Phormium tenax* 'Variegatum').

◄ **Summer blaze** The impressive orange trumpets of a Mid-Century Hybrid lily reach forward among a sea of bright yellow, summer-blooming *Lysimachia punctata*. The yellow-green flowers and soft foliage of *Alchemilla mollis* (lady's mantle) cool the fire of this grouping.

▼ **Green verges** Lady's mantle (*Alchemilla mollis*) is ideal for border edging and in flower arrangements. Throughout summer, the leafy clumps are topped with billowing sprays of yellow-green, long-lasting flowers.

▲ **Yellow summer border** Drifts of ox-eye chamomile (*Anthemis tinctoria*), with pale yellow daisy blooms, merge into robust Jerusalem sage (*Phlomis fruticosa*) studded with whorls of hooded golden-yellow flowers.

▲ **Orange and yellow** The intense orange colour of *Geum × borisii* needs careful siting in the strong sun of high summer. A group of dwarf, bright yellow evening primroses (*Oenothera missouriensis*) provides the perfect cooling effect, further helped by a backing of the elegant, dark green foliage of stinking hellebore (*Helleborus foetidus*).

◄ **Autumn layers** Red-hot pokers – not all of which are red – like *Kniphofia* 'Bee's Lemon' give eye-catching vertical interest to an early autumn scene. They are partnered by the brown-centred, golden-orange daisy flowers of *Helenium autumnale* and backed by crimson-purple spikes of *Salvia × superba*. In the foreground, the flat heads of *Sedum × 'Autumn Joy'* are still yellow-green.

▲ **Drops of gold** In early autumn, the evergreen shrub *Bupleurum fruticosum* becomes an airy cloudbank of delicate, fennel-yellow flowers gathered in rounded heads. Prized by flower arrangers, they also provide a graceful background for the primrose-yellow blooms of the tender *Chrysanthemum frutescens*.

► **Yellow goblets** Autumn-flowering *Sternbergia lutea* opens its waxy yellow goblets wide at the touch of late-summer sun. Native to scorched Mediterranean scrubland, these small bulbs revel in warmth and shelter in the company of other inhabitants of that region, such as silver-grey lavender (*Lavandula*) and semi-evergreen *Euphorbia characias wulfenii* with blue-grey leaf whorls.

YELLOW THROUGH THE YEAR · **YELLOW AND ORANGE FLOWERS**

◄ **Autumn mists** Set against a background of hazy silver-grey *Artemisia absinthium* 'Lambrook Silver', groups of yellow, golden and bronze spray chrysanthemums bring colour to the autumn border. They reflect the slanting rays of a lowering sun and the tints in autumn foliage, but their radiance is extinguished with the first touch of frost.

▼ **Winter sun** In the pale sunshine of late winter, tiny winter aconites (*Eranthis hyemalis*) spread out their lemon-yellow flower cups above ruffs of pale green leaves. They carpet the ground beneath the bare, coral-red stems of *Cornus alba* 'Sibirica' and, on the left, a shrubby willow (*Salix irrorata*) whose purple stems, overlaid with white bloom, are closely set with catkins about to burst at any moment.

▲ Winter curios The spiralling and twisted shoots of the corkscrew hazel (*Corylus avellana* 'Contorta') are particularly noticeable in their bare winter profile. Early in the year, yellow catkins droop from every curious bend and angle to shed their pollen over an underplanting bright with colour from *Crocus* 'Golden Bunch' and drifts of dwarf blue *Iris histrioides*.

▼ Winter into spring The evergreen Corsican hellebore (*Helleborus lividus corsicus*) is unpredictable. The huge clusters of lime-green, cup-like flowers may open as early as December or as late as May. In most years, though, the stout flower stems above thick, leathery and spiny leaves come into their full glory in mid spring, at the same time as the little lungwort (*Pulmonaria officinalis*) with spotted leaves and pinkish-purple blooms comes into flower.

▲ Golden summer In this pretty association, the yellow flowers of the sub-shrubby *Chrysanthemum frutescens* 'Jamaica Primrose' are echoed by the fascinating gold-marked foliage of *Iresine herbstii* 'Aureo-reticulata'.

◄ First rose of summer The clear yellow blooms of *Rosa ecae* 'Helen Knight', set among fine, fern-like leaves, open in late spring. They tone down the hot orange colours of wallflowers and complement the large lemon-yellow cups of the fleetingly beautiful *Paeonia mlokosewitschii*.

YELLOW AND ORANGE-COLOURED FLOWERS

	NAME	DESCRIPTION/SITE	HEIGHT	SEASON
SHRUBS	Berberis darwinii	Evergreen, autumn berries; any soil, sun	2.4-3m (8-10ft)	Spring
	Buddleia globosa	Evergreen; loamy soil, sun	3m (10ft)	Spring-summer
	Callistemon salignus	Half-hardy evergreen; any soil, sun/shelter	1.5-2.4m (5-8ft)	Summer
	Chimonanthus praecox	Deciduous; ordinary soil, sun/wall shelter	3m (10ft)	Winter
	Colutea arborescens	Deciduous, attractive seed pods; light soil, sun	2.4-3m (8-10ft)	Summer-autumn
	Cornus mas	Deciduous; ordinary soil, sun	2.4-3.6m (8-12ft)	Winter-spring
	Coronilla emerus	Deciduous; ordinary soil, sun/shelter	2.4m (8ft)	Spring
	Corylopsis sp.	Deciduous; lime-free soil, sun	1.5-3m (5-10ft)	Winter-spring
	Corylus avellana 'Contorta'	Deciduous, twisted stems and leaves; well-drained soil, sun	to 1.8m (6ft)	Winter
	Cytisus battandieri, C. scoparius	Deciduous; any soil, sun	2.4-3m (8-10ft)	Late spring-summer
	Forsythia sp. and vars.	Deciduous; any soil, sun/light shade	1.2-3m (4-10ft)	Spring
	Genista sp.	Deciduous; any soil, sun	60-120cm (2-4ft)	Late spring-summer
	Halemium ocymoides	Evergreen, compact; light soil, sun/shelter	60-90cm (2-3ft)	Early summer
	Helianthemum nummularium vars.	Evergreen; ordinary soil, sun	10-15cm (4-6in)	Summer
	Hamamelis sp. and vars.	Deciduous; moist acid soil, sun/shelter	1.8-3m (6-10ft)	Winter
	Hypericum calycinum	Semi-evergreen; any soil, sun	30-45cm (1-1½ft)	Summer-autumn
	Jasminum nudiflorum	Deciduous; ordinary soil, sun/shade	3m (10ft)	Winter
	Kerria japonica	Deciduous; ordinary soil, sun/shade	1.8-3.6m (6-12ft)	Spring
	Laburnum sp.	Deciduous trees; ordinary soil, sun/shade	1.8-6m (6-20ft)	Late spring
	Lindera benzoin	Deciduous, autumn tints; moist lime-free soil, light shade	2.4m (8ft)	Spring
	Lonicera periclymenum vars.	Deciduous climbers; ordinary soil, sun/shade	4.5-6m (15-20ft)	Summer
	Lupinus arboreus	Deciduous, elegant foliage; light soil, sun	60-120cm (2-4ft)	Summer
	Mahonia sp. and vars.	Evergreen; rich soil, light shade	1.5-3m (5-10ft)	Winter
	Paeonia x lemonei, P. lutea	Deciduous; rich soil, sun/shelter	1.2-1.8m (4-6ft)	Spring-summer
	Phlomis fruticosa	Evergreen; light soil, sun	0.9-1.2m (3-4ft)	Summer
	Potentilla fruticosa vars.	Deciduous; light soil, sun	90cm (3ft)	Summer-autumn
	Senecio 'Sunshine'	Evergreen, grey-leaved; well-drained soil, sun	90cm (3ft)	Summer
	Sophora tetraptera	Evergreen, near hardy; fertile soil, sun/shelter	3.5m (12ft)	Spring
	Spartium junceum	Deciduous; any soil, sun	2.4-3m (8-10ft)	Summer-autumn
	Ulex europaeus	Evergreen; any and poor soil; sun	1.5-1.8m (5-6ft)	Spring-autumn
ANNUALS	Antirrhinum 'Yellow Monarch'	Half-hardy; rich soil, sun/light shade	38-45cm (15-18in)	Summer-autumn
	Argemone mexicana	Hardy; light soil, sun	60cm (2ft)	Summer
	Calceolaria integrifolia	Half-hardy; lime-free soil, sun/shelter	30-38cm (12-15in)	Summer-autumn
	Calendula officinalis vars.	Hardy; any even poor soil; sun/shade	30-60cm (1-2ft)	Spring-autumn
	Celosia cristata 'Golden Triumph'	Half-hardy; well-drained soil, sun/shelter	60cm (2ft)	Summer-autumn
	Dimorphotheca aurantiaca vars.	Half-hardy; light soil, sun	30-45cm (1-1½ft)	Summer-autumn
	Eschscholzia californica	Half-hardy; poor soil, sun	12-38cm (5-15in)	Summer-autumn
	Gazania x hybrida	Half-hardy; light soil, sun	23cm (9in)	Summer-autumn
	Helichrysum vars.	Half-hardy everlastings; light soil, sun	0.9-1.2m (3-4ft)	Summer
	Layia elegans	Hardy; sandy soil, sun	45cm (1½ft)	Summer-autumn
	Limnanthes douglasii	Hardy; any soil, sun	15cm (6in)	Spring-summer
	Matricaria eximia 'Golden Ball'	Half-hardy; light soil, sun	30cm (1ft)	Summer
	Mentzelia lindleyi	Hardy; light soil, sun	45cm (1½ft)	Spring
	Petunia 'Brass Band'	Half-hardy Multifloras; well-drained soil, sun	30cm (1ft)	Summer-autumn
	Tagetes sp. and vars.	Half-hardy; any soil, sun	15-90cm (6-36in)	Summer-autumn
	Thunbergia alata	Hardy climber; any soil, sun and shelter	3m (10ft)	Summer-autumn
	Tropaeolum majus vars.	Hardy; poor soil, sun	23-38cm (9-15in)	Summer-autumn
	Ursinia anethoides	Half-hardy, ferny foliage; light soil, sun	45cm (1½ft)	Summer-autumn
	Venidium fastuosum	Half-hardy; light soil, sun	60cm (2ft)	Summer-autumn

BORDER PLANTS

NAME	DESCRIPTION/SITE	HEIGHT	SEASON
Achillea sp. and vars.	Ferny foliage; any soil, sun	0.9-1.2m (3-4ft)	Summer
Aconitum 'Ivorine'	Handsome foliage; deep moist soil, partial shade	90cm (3ft)	Late spring-summer
Adonis amurensis	Fine leaves; any soil, sun/shade	23-38cm (9-15in)	Winter-spring
Alyssum saxatile	Evergreen trailer; any soil, sun	5-30cm (2-12in)	Spring-summer
Allium moly	Bulbous; any soil, sun	30cm (1ft)	Summer
Alstroemeria autantiaca	Bulbous; rich soil, sun and shelter	60-90cm (2-3ft)	Summer
Anthemis tinctoria	Ferny foliage; any soil, sun	75cm (2½ft)	Summer
Centaurea macrocephala	Thistle-like; any soil, sun	1.8m (6ft)	Summer
Chrysogonum virginianum	Dense bright green foliage; lime-free soil, sun/light shade	30-60cm (1-2ft)	Spring-autumn
Coreopsis sp. and vars.	Easy-growing; light soil, sun	30-60cm (1-2ft)	Summer
Corydalis lutea	Handsome leaves; any soil, sun/shade	30cm (1ft)	Spring-autumn
Crocosmia masonorum	Sword-shaped leaves; light soil, sun	60-75cm (2-2½ft)	Summer
Crocus sp. and vars.	Well-drained soil, sun/light shade	7.5-12cm (3-5in)	Winter-spring
Digitalis grandiflora, D. lutea	Hairy leaves; moist soil, light shade	30-90cm (1-3ft)	Late spring-summer
Doronicum sp. and vars.	Heart-shaped leaves; moist soil, sun	20-90cm (8-36in)	Spring-early summer
Draba sp.	Evergreen, hummock-forming; well-drained soil, sun	2.5-10cm (1-4in)	Spring-early summer
Eranthis sp.	Tuberous; loamy soil, sun/light shade	10cm (4in)	Winter-spring
Erigeron aurantiacus	Mat-forming; moist soil, sun	25cm (10in)	Summer
Erysimum alpinum	Rock garden plant; poor soil, sun	15cm (6in)	Spring-summer
Erythronium tuolumnense	Clump-forming; moist soil, light shade	23-30cm (9-12in)	Spring
Euphorbia sp.	Handsome foliage/bracts; any soil, sun	0.6-1.2m (2-4ft)	Spring-summer
Fritillaria imperialis	Bulbous; loamy soil, sun/light shade	60-90cm (2-3ft)	Late spring
Gaillardia vars.	Grey-green foliage; light soil, sun	25-75cm (10-30in)	Summer-autumn
Gentiana lutea	Whorls of veined leaves; rich moist soil, sun/light shade	to 1.5m (5ft)	Summer
Geum sp. and vars.	Border and rock plants; rich soil, sun/light shade	15-30cm (6-12in)	Spring-autumn
Helenium autumnale vars.	Branching; any soil, sun	1.2-1.8m (4-6ft)	Summer-autumn
Helianthus sp. and vars.	Perennials/annuals; any soil, sun	1.2-1.8m (4-6ft)	Summer-autumn
Heliopsis scabra	Single and double vars; any soil, sun	0.9-1.2m (3-4ft)	Summer
Hieracium villosum	Rosette-forming, grey foliage; any, poor soil, sun	30cm (1ft)	Summer
Inula sp.	Rock/border plants; moist soil, sun	10-60cm (4-24in)	Spring-autumn
Kniphofia vars.	Clump-forming; any soil, sun	0.6-1.8m (2-6ft)	Summer-autumn
Ligularia sp.	Large-leaved; moist soil, light shade	0.9-1.8m (3-6ft)	Summer
Lysimachia punctata	Easy-grown; moist soil, sun/light shade	90cm (3ft)	Summer
Meconopsis cambrica	Ferny leaves; any soil, sun/light shade	30-45cm (1-1½ft)	Summer-autumn
Mimulus guttatus	Ultra hardy; moist soil, sun/light shade	60cm (2ft)	Late sping-autumn
Oenothera sp.	Border/rock plants; light soil, sun	10-90cm (4-36in)	Summer-autumn
Paeonia lactiflora vars.	Handsome foliage; moist soil, sun/light shade	75-90cm (2½-3ft)	Early summer
Papaver pyrenaicum	Finely cut foliage; gritty well-drained soil, sun	25cm (10in)	Summer
Pulsatilla alpina sulphurea	Ferny leaves; rich soil, sun	30cm (1ft)	Late spring
Ranunculus sp. and vars.	Bright green leaves; moist soil, sun/shade	15-75cm (6-30in)	Spring-summer
Roscoea cautleoides	Sword-shaped leaves; moisture-retentive soil, sun/shade	38-45cm (15-18in)	Summer
Rudbeckia sp. and vars.	Spreading; any soil, sun	0.6-2.1m (2-7ft)	Summer-autumn
Saxifraga x *elizabethae*	Mat-forming; rich soil, sun/light shade	7.5cm (3in)	Spring
Sedum aizoon, S. rosea	Glossy foliage; any soil, sun	30cm (1ft)	Late spring-summer
Solidago sp. and vars.	Invasive; any soil, sun	0.9-1.8m (3-6ft)	Summer-autumn
Sternbergia lutea	Bulbous; well-drained soil, sun/shelter	10-15cm (4-6in)	Autumn
Tigridia pavonia	Bulbous, half-hardy; well-drained soil, shelter	40-45cm (16-18in)	Summer-autumn
Trollius sp.	Divided foliage; moist soil, sun/light shade	30-75cm (1-2½ft)	Spring-summer
Veratrum viride	Large ribbed and pleated leaves; moist soil, light shade	2.1m (7ft)	Summer
Verbascum sp.	Imposing plants; any soil, sun	to 1.8m (6ft)	Late spring-autumn
Waldsteinia ternata	Evergreen and mat-forming; moist soil, sun/light shade	10cm (4in)	Spring

Pink and red flowers

Pink is a warm and friendly colour, associated with the romance and charm of sweetly-scented old fashioned gardens, especially in spring and summer. It is the colour of flowering cherries, primulas and Japanese quinces, of roses and peonies, garden pinks and sweet peas. It is also one of the many vibrant autumn colours – in the soft pink shades of colchicums and nerines – and the winter scene has displays of bright shades of pink in the heather garden, and in the unsurpassed beauty of clear pink and bright red camellia blooms.

Pink and red hues range from pink-tinged white to clear candyfloss, and from rich cerise to scarlet, crimson and magenta, which merge into shades of purple and blue. There are the dusky pinks of eupatoriums, the vivid scarlet of bedding salvias, the salmon or coral-red of honeysuckles, and the reddish-brown of some autumn sedums. The paler the pink, the more luminous it appears, particularly against dark backgrounds. Conversely, dark pinks and strident reds seem to vanish at dusk and need the cooling effects of grey, silver or blue-green foliage to help to bring them back into focus.

Pale pink schemes can look sugary and insipid, and are all but lost in bright sunshine unless they are contrasted with stronger shades. To be really effective, a monochromatic planting scheme should include a range of mixes, tints and nuances of the basic colour. Planting schemes should also take account of the different flower shapes and textures, heights and growth patterns, and move almost imperceptibly through harmonizing hues and contrasting forms, setting pale colours against slightly darker ones, rigid shapes against airy profiles and silky petals against stiff bracts.

An abundance of roses Climbers and shrub roses jostle in glorious summer colours.

PINK PERFECTION

**Pink flowers provide restful warmth
and subtle elegance for any garden – effects
often enhanced by foliage colour.**

In distinct contrast to warm yellows and cool blues, shades of pink generate a soft and nostalgic atmosphere – the essence of the traditional cottage garden style.

Pastel pinks glow in evening light when darker hues are disappearing into the shadows. They appear deeper when integrated with silvery-white foliage, somewhat redder when seen against greens, and more vivid among greys. By day, pinks are less eye-catching than the stronger colours, but serve to mellow the impact of bold architectural plants.

Many a pink flower reveals exceptional beauty of form when seen close up. A tracery of mauve or purple veins may enhance the ground colour, a centre of golden stamens can add lustre, or finely divided petals may give a lacy softness of texture.

For late-winter warmth, there are the many camellias. When frosts, mists and snow cause pale colours to merge into obscurity, their green, glossy leaves are the perfect background for their stunning flowers.

Heralding the spring, flowering almonds burst forth with soft pink flowers before any real suspicion of greenery joins them on the bare twigs. With the related flowering cherries, the pink flower effect is often heightened by purplish or bronze young foliage. Underplantings of the pink-flowered *Anemone blanda* and groupings with viburnums complete the effect.

Mid to late spring is associated with the vivacious yellows and reds of daffodils and tulips, but there are many pink flowers, too. The tulip-like flowers of the common magnolia, billowy sprays

▲ **Old-fashioned pinks** The deliciously scented Bourbon rose 'Mme Isaac Pereire' bears huge, cerise-pink blooms in early summer – and again in autumn. It is accompanied by pink hybrids of *Paeonia lactiflora*.

▼ **Cottage-garden charm** An all-pink theme includes a broad rim of *Aubrieta deltoidea* 'Riverslea', containers of rhododendrons and evergreen azaleas and tall-growing columbines (*Aquilegia* × *hybrida*).

of pink deciduous azaleas and suckering clumps of the rose-pink dwarf Russian almond (*Prunus tenella*) look marvellous alongside drifts of woodland primulas, dog's-tooth violets and bergenias. For a beautiful scrambling backdrop choose *Clematis montana* varieties such as 'Elizabeth' or 'Rubens', or *C. macropetala* 'Markham's Pink'.

Summer pink effects are many and varied – from hazy seas of *Geranium endressii* or *Gypsophila paniculata* 'Rosy Veil' to the statuesque elegance of *Cleome* 'Rose Queen' or perennial foxgloves (*Digitalis* × *mertonensis*). Silver-leaved plants come to a peak in summer and are brought to life by sharper pink shades – some of the petunias, for instance.

From late summer through to autumn, warm tones of orange and bronze predominate, yet there are many surprises. Belladonna lilies (*Amaryllis belladonna*), *Cyclamen hederifolium*, autumn-flowering crocuses (*Crocus kotschyanus* for example) and colchicums are all excellent for underplanting in groups or informal drifts – perhaps under the pink-fruited shrub *Euonymus yedoensis* 'Coral Charm'.

▲ **Autumn pinks** Single-flowered, pale pink spray chrysanthemums backed by massed clumps of deeper pink Japanese anemones (*Anemone* × *hybrida*) provide welcome relief in autumn borders where fiery orange and bronze colours usually predominate at the close of the growing season.

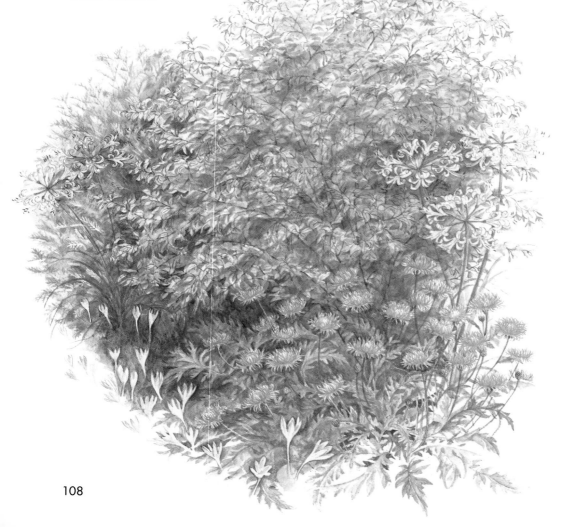

◄ **Shades of pink** In September and October, the South African *Nerine bowdenii* raises tall leafless stems topped with huge, elegant clusters of satiny, glowing pink flowers. The stems are hidden by clumps of deep rose-pink cornflowers (*Centaurea dealbata* 'John Coutts'), with grey-green, deeply divided foliage, and by pale pink goblets of the autumn crocus (*Colchicum autumnale*). Complementing the autumn scene is a 1.2m (4ft) tall *Fuchsia magellanica* 'Versicolor', dripping pink and purple blooms from its variegated foliage of grey, green and pink.

▲ **Pink and white** Mezereon (*Daphne mezereum*) begins to flower in late winter, wreathing its bare branches in exquisitely scented blooms of rose to purple-pink. An early-spring association could include *Crocus sieberi* 'Firefly' and white and pink *Anemone blanda*.

▲ **Pink and scarlet** The native yarrow (*Achillea millefolium*) is the parent of many fine border plants, including the cherry-pink 'Cerise Queen' whose large flat flower heads contrast well with the dark green feathery foliage. In high summer, it brings splashes of bright colour to herbaceous borders, particularly vivid in the company of the taller *Penstemon × gloxiniodes* hybrids whose tubular flowers glow crimson-scarlet.

◄ **Pink and peach** The 'Excelsior' strain of the common foxglove (*Digitalis purpurea*) includes a range of pure colours – pink, apricot, peach and white. The 1.5m (5ft) tall flower stems, thoroughly at home in cottage and wild gardens, tower above deep pink rugosa roses and the deeper red flower clusters of the evergreen *Escallonia macrantha*.

▶ **Pink annuals** Many annuals and biennials are sold in strains of mixed colours, but just as many are available in single shades. Snapdragons (*Antirrhinum*) and tobacco plants (*Nicotiana*) both come in named colour selections. Here, rose-pink snapdragons and cerise nicotianas are bedded out round the perennial, pink-flowered yarrow *Achillea millefolium* 'Red Beauty'.

▼ **Red as roses** A large-scale planting of evergreen rhododendrons is smothered in late spring with huge heads of deep pink blooms. Their colour and form are repeated in the wide-spreading but smaller-flowered azalea (*Rhododendron obtusum* 'Amoenum'). The same stunning colour effect can be achieved in small gardens with dwarf rhododendron and azalea hybrids.

PINK AND WHITE

Delicate combinations of pink and white flowers gain strength and visual impact when partnered with bold fresh green foliage plants.

Pink and white make a lovely team. Pink shows up well in the diffused light of overcast days and towards dusk while white brings freshness during the day and excels as night approaches.

Green foliage, whether evergreen or deciduous, and the subtlety of green flowers play an important role in strengthening pink and white partnerships when the various shades and tints and the textures and shapes are brought into play.

For example, bring brightness to a winter garden with groups of pink and white winter heath (*Erica carnea*) planted around narrow conifers whose foliage tints range from the deepest green to blue-green and golden-green.

For spring partnerships, plant white narcissi in grass beneath a pink-flowering cherry tree. On a more intimate scale, the American trout lily (*Erythronium revolutum* 'White Beauty') with mottled green foliage associates well with *Anemone blanda* 'Pink Star' which has lobed, deeply cut leaves accentuating the starry form of its flowers. The large leathery leaves of *Bergenia* 'Silberlicht' make a striking foliage contrast while its silvery pink blooms complement the flowers of both partners.

White roses, such as the glossy leaved 'Iceberg', look even better when underplanted with the deeply cut, mid green leaves and pink flowers of *Geranium endressii* 'Wargrave Pink'. The climber *Actinidia kolomikta* could intro-

duce vertical interest behind, its unusual pink, green and white foliage continuing the pretty colour theme.

In autumn, try the lilac-pink goblets of *Colchicum autumnale*, pink and white forms of *Cyclamen hederifolium* and, for foliage ground cover, the bold variegated green and white of ivy (*Hedera helix* 'Eva'). Such pink, green and white combinations introduce a lovely fresh note to the garden in autumn.

▼ **Pink, green and white** In spring, a corner of a wild garden is a joyful combination of clear colours. The fluffy white plumes of *Smilacina racemosa* shimmer against red-flowered broom (*Cytisus scoparius* 'Burkwoodii'), pink rhododendrons and green conifer colours.

▲ Spring companions The pink-flowered thrift (*Armeria maritima*) shows up the dainty white sprays of St Bernard's lily (*Anthericum liliago*) in late spring. Both have grassy leaves that contrast attractively in colour.

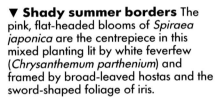

▼ Shady summer borders The pink, flat-headed blooms of *Spiraea japonica* are the centrepiece in this mixed planting lit by white feverfew (*Chrysanthemum parthenium*) and framed by broad-leaved hostas and the sword-shaped foliage of iris.

▲ Ornamental onions The large *Allium* family includes the tall *A. sphaerocephalum*, with its tightly packed purple-pink globes. Here they are planted with the white clusters of *A. neapolitanum* and the rose-coloured *A. oreophilum* var. *ostrowskianum*.

▶ Pink accents The fingered leaves of a Japanese acer provide a handsome backdrop for the pink bottlebrush spikes of knotweed (*Polygonum bistorta* 'Superba') rising above white *Chrysanthemum frutescens* and white-variegated hostas.

▲ **Winter cheer** In late winter this little pastel-coloured group creates an unforgettable picture. Soft pink cups of the Lenten rose (*Helleborus orientalis* 'Winter Cheer') rise above the broad spear-shaped, glossy green leaves of *Arum italicum* 'Pictum' marbled cream and grey. In their shade snowdrops (*Galanthus nivalis*) gently nod their white bells.

▲ **Summer tints** A semi-wild corner of a herbaceous border is filled with old-fashioned herbs. At the back are the much branched spikes of the 1.2m (4ft) tall biennial clary (*Salvia sclarea*) closely decked with pinkish-white flowers.

The pink theme is repeated in the large soft pink flowers of the peony 'Bowl of Beauty' and in the smaller cerise blooms of crane's-bill (*Geranium psilostemon*). The airy group is given form and substance by the enormous, deeply divided and aromatic leaves of angelica (*Angelica archangelica*) rising from a froth of white feverfew (*Chrysanthemum parthenium*).

◄ **Sweet alyssum** Correctly known as *Lobularia maritima*, this little annual spreads its white carpets far and wide during the summer.

White is also the colour of the double-flowered form of *Chrysanthemum parthenium*, whose button-like blooms are held above fern-like foliage, and the bowl shaped flowers of another annual, *Lavatera trimestris* 'Mont Blanc'.

At the back of this planting are the pink and white of flowering tobacco (*Nicotiana*), freshened by the subtle colouring of the cultivar 'Lime Green'.

◄ **Summer tapestry** One of the joys of annuals is their long-lasting display of colour. Candytuft (*Iberis umbellata*) is deservedly popular, carrying its blend of white, pink, lavender and pale mauve flower heads in a spreading colour tapestry. It is woven through with the similarly coloured *Clarkia elegans* that provides contrast of form with their taller and slender spikes.

▼ **Late-summer symphony** By August the herbaceous border can look dingy where early perennials have died back. Easy annuals fill such gaps to perfection, bringing a new freshness to permanent occupants. The profusely flowering mallow (*Lavatera trimestris*) with its wide rose-pink funnels mingles with heavily scented, pastel-hued tobacco plants (*Nicotiana alata*) and the deeper pink heads of perennial *Phlox paniculata*.

Late-summer harmony Pink *Dicentra eximia* blends with blue lavender and *Echinops ritro*.

PINK AND BLUE

Bright or misty blues and dark or pale pinks combine to form partnerships of subtle contrasts and muted harmony.

When blue and red are placed side by side they often jar, presenting a restless association. If pink is used instead of red, however, a partnership with blue becomes not only possible but highly pleasing – the two colours harmonize and at the same time offer sufficient contrast to retain individual interest. This point is well illustrated in such typical bedding schemes as pale pink tulips among a sea of forget-me-nots in preference to scarlet tulips among crisp blue muscaris.

Dark blue, as found in veronicas and some irises and delphiniums, can appear distinctly sombre but this mood is easily lifted if you grow pale pink flowers alongside. The introduction of pale pink will also make the blue stand out in fading light or a shady corner.

Bringing plants together in an attractive combination of hues is not just a matter of getting the colours right. Quantity is also important, one of the main rules being that there should always be larger drifts of the softer than the stronger colour.

Bear in mind, also, that a group's visual appeal will be increased if you use contrasting flower forms. For example, set the frothy blue flowers of ceanothus against the bold pink blooms of a climbing rose such as 'Pink Perpetué'. Or in moist semi-shaded conditions, combine the rose-pink candelabra-flowered *Primula pulverulenta* hybrids alongside the saucer-shaped blooms of the Himalayan blue poppy (*Meconopsis betonicifolia*).

▲ **High-summer partners** Pink bowl-shaped *Sidalcea malviflora* 'Loveliness' forms a soft foil for the metallic blues of spiky *Eryngium* × *oliverianum*.

▼ **Midsummer mists** The impact of the rich blue sprays of *Anchusa azurea* is perfectly toned down by a deep pink peony, pink and rose-red foxgloves (*Digitalis purpurea*) and stately spikes of lavender-blue delphiniums.

▶ **Summer annuals** Half-hardy begonias (*Begonia semperflorens*) flower incessantly from May until October or November. With their glossy green or purple leaves and deep pink flowers, they make handsome low-growing companions for the taller *Salvia farinacea* 'Victoria' whose vivid purple-blue spikes are softened by the pale pink of penstemon hybrids.

◀ **Froth of pink** The hardy deciduous shrub *Weigela florida* 'Variegata' is as delightful in leaf as it is in bloom. In mid spring the young leaves unfold pink, white and pale green. By high summer they have matured to dark green edged with lime-green but before that happens, the shrub is dressed with foxglove-like, pink and white flowers.

Blue *Iris pallida dalmatica* are planted in front, contrasting in colour and upright form with the informality of the weigela, and intermingle with loose sprays of the white-flowered honesty (*Lunaria annua* 'Alba').

► **Forget-me-not blue** *Anchusa azurea* 'Loddon Royalist' is one of the few pure blue flowers of summer. Branched flower panicles are borne on 90cm (3ft) tall stems well above the rather coarse basal leaves that are best hidden from view. Here, in midsummer, the gap is filled by clumps of pink and red, white-eyed sweet Williams (*Dianthus barbatus*), accompanied by the yellow-green froth of lady's mantle (*Alchemilla mollis*).

▼ **Springtime shade**
The evergreen *Bergenia* 'Ballawley' thrives in the moist soil and dappled shade of a woodland setting. Its fuchsia-red bell flowers perfectly match a flowering azalea and startlingly punctuate a carpet of Spanish bluebells (*Scilla campanulata*).

▲ **Roses all the way** The little polyantha rose 'The Fairy' flowers continuously through summer and autumn, with tiny double, clear pink blooms. In this herbaceous border, it is partnered with blue larkspurs (*Delphinium consolida*).

▲ **Summer contrasts** Soft cerise-pink flower clusters of *Phlox paniculata* serve as a foil for the imposing white and purple spikes of bear's breeches (*Acanthus spinosus*). Colour contrast is introduced with a planting of globe thistles (*Echinops ritro*) carrying perfect globes of steel-blue.

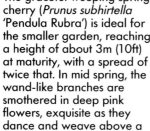

▶ **Splendour in spring** The graceful weeping spring cherry (*Prunus subhirtella* 'Pendula Rubra') is ideal for the smaller garden, reaching a height of about 3m (10ft) at maturity, with a spread of twice that. In mid spring, the wand-like branches are smothered in deep pink flowers, exquisite as they dance and weave above a cover of blue *Scilla sibirica*.

SCARLET & CRIMSON

Flowers in eye-catching reds may take over a garden, but used with discretion they can form harmonious pictures.

Red is a powerful and sometimes even aggressive colour, which can make it tricky to handle in the garden. As a general rule it should be used in small doses at all times.

Beds of all-red flowers invariably look best if they have plenty of green or grey foliage plants in them. Make sure these foliage plants take up more room than the flowers, because too much red, even when coupled with green or grey, will tire the eyes.

If you want to partner red with other flower colours – blue and yellow, perhaps – choose the paler hues. Mixed with royal blue or bright yellow, the combination jars.

A clever way of incorporating full-blooded red into a mixed border is to lead the eye gently towards it, along a trail of flowers with a hint of red in them.

The siting of red also requires careful consideration. In good light, red gives an impression of coming towards the viewer. Thus a clump of red flowers at the far end of the lawn will make a garden seem shorter – something only gardeners with long narrow plots would want. Secondly, red flowers do not show up well in evening light; for patio decoration they should always be mixed with pale flower colours.

▲ **Colour continuity** The dusky red velvety blooms of the Gallica rose 'Tuscany Superb' are mellowed by the sky-blue flowers of climbing morning glory (*Ipomoea tricolor*).

▼ **Pale companions** Yellow verbascums, flat-headed yarrows (*Achillea*) and pale day lilies (*Hemerocallis*) brighten a crimson and scarlet group of roses, dahlias, penstemons and nicotianas.

▲ **Postbox-red** The soft, silvery-grey foliage and rambling stems of the tender *Helichrysum petiolatum* frame and subdue containers brimming with the brilliant red trumpet flowers of bedding petunias.

▶ **Snowflakes in spring** Scarlet tulip goblets glow against a backdrop of fresh green spring foliage. Their intense colour is cooled by the variegated leaves and white flowers of honesty (*Lunaria annua* 'Variegata Alba') and the delicate white bells of the summer snowflake (*Leocujum aestivum*) which, in spite of its name, flowers during the spring.

◀ **Summer support** In summer, the deciduous shrub *Viburnum × bodnantense* is dull green but an excellent host and support for the vigorous *Clematis viticella* 'Royal Velours' which weaves its stems and nodding red flowers through the dense greenery. Shading the clematis roots are clumps of blue bellflowers (*Campanula persicifolia*) and early-flowering *Allium albopilosum* whose seed heads remain attractive for months.

The high point for this shrub is during the winter, when it flowers abundantly.

122

▼ **Summer partners** The herbaceous perennials in this elegant grouping perfectly complement and contrast with each other in colour and form. A clump of vermilion-red Oriental poppies (*Papaver orientale*), with petals like crumpled silk, flops hairy stems in front of erect spires of pink, red and blue Russell lupins. The foliage of both poppies and lupins contrasts strongly with the bold glossy leaves of a blue-green hosta. As summer progresses, the hosta will hide the gap left by the lupins, and the poppy flowers will be replaced by decorative seed capsules.

In the background, a white-flowered clematis sheds light and airy grace over this early-summer picture.

▲ **Crowns of gold** The tall stems of crown imperials (*Fritillaria imperialis* 'Aurora') are topped with clusters of drooping orange-yellow bell flowers. They make unusual but magnificent companions for the scarlet trumpets of dwarf rhododendrons in late spring.

▶ Study in purple
Brilliant red evergreen azaleas (far right) and lower-growing rhododendrons (front) are separated by a purple-leaved *Berberis thunbergii* 'Atropurpurea Nana'. At flowering time in late spring, a white broom (*Cytisus × praecox* 'Alba') brings relief to the sombre composition. During the summer its green, wand-like stems contrast effectively with both the leathery rhododendron leaves and the purple berberis.

▼ Flowers of the field
The blood red *Anemone coronaria* is thought by some authorities to be the plant referred to in the biblical phrase 'flowers of the field'. It naturalizes easily in short grass and looks even more startling in the company of its smaller-flowered, pale blue relation, *Anemone blanda*.

PINK THROUGH THE YEAR

There are shades of pink to match every season, from pale spring blossom to the red of summer fuchsia and the purple-pink autumn crocus.

Early spring comes to the rock garden with pink fairy foxgloves (*Erinus alpinus*) and mossy saxifrages; it bursts forth with cherry blossom and pink-stained magnolia chalices, with deep pink hyacinths and scarlet tulips. Later still is the stupendous floral display of the rhododendrons and azaleas in every conceivable shade of pink and red. But most of all, these colours belong to the summer garden, the tones growing steadily deeper towards true red.

There is a vast number of pink summer-flowering shrubs, from the evergreen *Abelia* × *grandiflora* with pink and white funnels, and heady-scented lilacs (*Syringa* 'Marechal Foch'), to the drooping clusters of pea-like blooms on *Robinia hispida*, or the ground-hugging little rock rose, such as *Helianthemum nummularium* 'Wisley Pink' massed with silky flowers the shape of single roses. The beauty bush (*Kolkwitzia amabilis*) is a fountain of porcelain-pink flowers that look like little foxgloves – they make a stunning early-summer partnership with a front planting of foxgloves proper (*Digitalis purpurea*).

Many of the favourite summer colours are in the pink colour range – fuchsias with their dainty bells, peonies, astilbes, bedding pelargoniums, salvias and petunias, and tasselled love-lies-bleeding. Roses, too, are an essential part of most summer gardens. Their variety is huge, from splendid old shrub roses like the pale pink 'Great Maidens Blush' to the deep pink of the more recent 'Silver Jubilee'.

Autumn means fiery red leaf tints and berry clusters, pale colchicums and *Cyclamen hederifolium*, and the exotic and iridescent flower heads of *Nerine bowdenii*. Winter is brightened with plants such as red-berried hollies, daphnes and camellias.

▼ **The essence of summer** A field of Oriental poppies (*Papaver orientale*) glows brilliant scarlet. Pink aquilegias and pale honesty (*Lunaria annua*) add cooler tones.

▲ **Cottage-garden charm** In the bright sun of high summer, the eye seeks the relief of cool colours. Complementary shades of pink provide such an oasis of calm, blending tall and wispy, pale pink clary (*Salvia sclarea*) with pink-flowered Canterbury bells (*Campanula medium*) and the quartered blooms of old-fashioned roses.

▲ **Bedding lobelias**
Perennial lobelias are quite different from the small blue-flowered annuals that decorate window boxes and hanging baskets in summer. The 1.2m (4ft) tall stems of *Lobelia cardinalis* 'Queen Victoria' are set with purple foliage and topped with spikes of vivid red flowers. Not reliably hardy, the clumps are best overwintered in a cold frame and planted out again in May.

▶ **Pink daisies** Low-growing fleabane (*Erigeron × hybridus*) thrives in sunny rock gardens and raised beds, opening yellow-centred, pink daisy flowers throughout summer. A close relative, *E. mucronatus*, with tiny white or pink flowers, is invasive, seeding itself in every crack and corner.

▲ Bowls of beauty The peony (*Paeonia lactiflora*) has been called queen among the perennials. Though the early-summer flowering season is short, it is more than compensated for by the magnificent bowl-shaped blooms in shades of pink, red or white. Peonies are almost invariably partnered with irises, the tall bearded types with blue, lilac or mauve flowers above elegant sword-shaped leaf fans.

◄ Autumn berries The evergreen *Cotoneaster* 'Hybridus Pendulus' makes a striking specimen tree for a lawn. Normally prostrate in form, it is often grafted on to an upright stem, to display weeping, glossy-leaved branches; in autumn and winter they are decked with an abundance of bright red berries.

▲ **Autumn crocus** The slender goblets of the little autumn crocus (*Colchicum agrippinum*) open during autumn to rosy-lilac stars. Their bright colour and naked stems demand some kind of muted foil, here supplied by the grey-green leaves and misty blue flower spikes of catmint (*Nepeta* × *faassenii*).

▲ **Glossy fruits** The red-tinted stems of the small evergreen shrub *Pernettya mucronata* are smothered in early summer with tiny white flowers that in autumn and winter become glistening clusters of jewel-like berries ranging in colour from white through pink and red to purple. For berries to be produced, male and female plants must be grown together — in lime-free soil.

◄ **Autumn dress** The common spindle tree (*Euonymus europaeus*) is a deciduous, vigorous shrub thriving in chalky soil. In autumn, the foliage assumes soft yellow tints, but the plant's real glory lies in the huge clusters of seed capsules. In the variety 'Red Cascade' they are rose-red and so abundant as to weigh down the branches.

◄ **Autumn into winter** Colour in the winter garden comes from evergreens, green or golden conifers as well as from shrubs with variegated leaves, spectacular berries or the unexpected bonus of flowers. The firethorns (*Pyracantha*) are among the most dependable berrying shrubs; the variety 'Mohave' has orange-red fruit which birds usually leave alone. Included in this cheerful winter scene is a silver-white variegated holly (*Ilex aquifolium* 'Ferox Argentea') and, on the right, *Viburnum tinus* showing off flat heads of pink-budded, white flowers among glossy leaves.

▼ **Spring growth** Rivalling the shrubby *Pieris* in splendour, the evergreen *Photinia* × *fraseri* 'Robusta' is ideal for gardeners on ordinary and alkaline soils. Given shelter and sun, the young growths unfold in spring like coppery-red candles that set the leathery dark green foliage blazing with colour.

▼ **Spring Japonicas** The familiar name of "Japonica" refers to the ornamental quince (*Chaenomeles speciosa*), from China. The variety 'Cardinalis' opens crimson-scarlet, saucer-shaped flowers in mid spring, at the same time as the first pale green leaves. By May, the shrub is in full glorious bloom, a focal point in this spring picture where clumps of yellow daisy flowers of *Doronicum plantagineum* 'Miss Mason' stand sentinel at either side.

At the front, *Euphorbia polychroma* creates smooth domes of brilliant yellow-green foliage and flower bracts.

▲ **Cherry blossom** The Japanese cherry *Prunus* 'Shirofugen' is one of the last ornamental cherries to bloom, in late spring. But the flowers are worth waiting for, creating a stunning canopy from long-stalked clusters of large double flowers. Purple-pink in bud, they open white only to fade eventually to purple-pink again. They contrast exquisitely with the coppery-red young leaves. Wide-spreading and up to 10m (30ft) tall, the cherry casts subtle highlights over a bold woodland planting of bright red azalea 'Sir William Lawrence'.

PINK AND RED-COLOURED FLOWERS

	NAME	DESCRIPTION/SITE	HEIGHT	SEASON
SHRUBS & TREES	Abelia x grandiflora	Semi-evergreen, bright green leaves; any soil, sun and shelter	1.5-2.4m (5-8ft)	Summer
	Andromeda polifolia	Evergreen, low-growing; acid moist soil, shade	45cm (1½ft)	Spring-summer
	Chaenomeles sp. and vars.	Deciduous, autumn fruit; any moist soil, sun	0.9-1.8m (3-6ft)	Spring
	Cistus x crispus 'Sunset', C. x purpureus	Evergreen, fairly hardy; poor soil, full sun	0.6-1.8m (2-6ft)	Summer
	Clethra alnifolia 'Rosea'	Deciduous; autumn tints; moist, lime-free soil, sun	1.8-2.4m (6-8ft)	Summer-autumn
	Cornus kousa	Deciduous, autumn tints; any well-drained soil, sun	3m (10ft)	Early summer
	Crataegus laevigata vars.	Deciduous trees, autumn haws; any soil, sun	5.5-7.5m (18-25ft)	Spring
	Daphne x burkwoodii	Evergreen; well-drained soil, sun/light shade	0.9-1.2m (3-4ft)	Spring-early summer
	D. cneorum	Evergreen; well-drained soil, sun/light shade	60-90cm (2-3ft)	Spring-early summer
	D. mezereum	Deciduous, upright; well-drained soil, sun	1.5m (5ft)	Winter
	Deutzia x elegantissima, D. x rosea	Deciduous, autumn tints; well-drained soil, sun	0.9-3m (3-10ft)	Late spring-summer
	Eccremocarpus scaber	Evergreen, near hardy climber; rich moist soil, sun, sheltered wall	2.4-3m (8-10ft)	Summer-autumn
	Escallonia hybrids	Evergreen, best in maritime gardens; well-drained soil, sun	1.5-2.4m (5-8ft)	Spring-autumn
	Helianthemum nummularium vars.	Evergreen, wide-spreading; well-drained soil, sun	5-15cm (2-6in)	Summer
	Indigofera sp.	Deciduous, near-hardy; rich soil, sun/shelter	1.5-3m (5-10ft)	Summer-autumn
	Kalmia latifolia	Evergreen, leathery leaves; moist acid soil, shade	0.9-3m (3-10ft)	Summer
	Kolkwitzia amabilis	Deciduous, thicket-forming; any soil, sun	1.8-3.6m (6-12ft)	Summer
	Lavatera olbia	Deciduous, near-hardy; any soil, sun/shelter	1.8-2.4m (6-8ft)	Summer-autumn
	Leycesteria formosa	Deciduous, autumn berries; any soil, sun/shade	1.8m (6ft)	Summer
	Lonicera periclymenum vars.	Deciduous climbers; well-drained soil, sun/shade	4.5-6m (15-20ft)	Summer-autumn
	L. sempervirens	Evergreen climber; loamy soil, sun/shelter	3-6m (10-20ft)	Summer
	Magnolia x soulangiana	Deciduous small tree; well-drained soil, sun	3-10m (10-33ft)	Spring
	M. x loebneri 'Leonard Messel'	Deciduous tree or shrub; lime-tolerant, sun	to 7.5m (25ft)	Early spring
	Malus floribunda, M. x purpurea	Deciduous trees, autumn fruit; any soil, sun	4.5m (15ft)	Spring
	Paeonia suffruticosa vars.	Deciduous, handsome foliage; rich soil, sun/shelter	1.2-1.8m (4-6ft)	Early summer
	Phyllodoce x intermedia	Evergreen sub-shrub; moist acid soil, cool shade	15-25cm (6-10in)	Early summer
	Potentilla fruticosa vars.	Deciduous, compact; light soil, sun	90cm (3ft)	Early summer-autumn
	Prunus sp. and vars.	Deciduous shrubs and trees; well-drained soil, sun	0.6-6m (2-20ft)	Late winter-spring
	Ribes sanguineum	Deciduous, easy; well-drained soil, sun/shade	1.8-2.4m (6-8ft)	Spring
	Robinia hispida	Deciduous, attractive foliage; well-drained soil, sun/shelter	1.8-2.4m (6-8ft)	Late spring-summer
	Spiraea x bumalda	Deciduous, wide-spreading; rich soil, sun	75-90cm (2½-3ft)	Summer
	Tropaeolum speciosum	Deciduous near-hardy climber; any well-drained soil, sun	4.5m (15ft)	Summer-early autumn
	Viburnum x bodnantense	Deciduous; bronze young leaves; moist soil, sun	2.7-3.6m (9-12ft)	Winter
	Weigela sp. and vars.	Deciduous, easy; well-drained soil, sun/light shade	1.5-1.8m (5-6ft)	Summer
ANNUALS	Adonis aestivalis	Hardy, fern-like leaves; any soil, sun/light shade	30cm (1ft)	Summer
	Agrostemma githago	Hardy, self-seeding; poor soil, sun	60-90cm (2-3ft)	Summer
	Callistephus chinensis	Half-hardy, good as cut flowers; any soil, sun	15-75cm (6-30in)	Summer-autumn
	Centaurea cyanus vars.	Hardy and easy; well-drained soil, sun	30-90cm (1-3ft)	Summer-autumn
	Clarkia elegans	Hardy, double-flowered; light soil, sun	30-60cm (1-2ft)	Summer-autumn
	Cosmos bipinnatus	Half-hardy, ferny leaves; poor soil, sun	60-90cm (2-3ft)	Summer-autumn
	Godetia grandiflora vars.	Hardy, bushy; well-drained soil, sun	23-50cm (9-20in)	Summer
	Gomphrena globosa vars.	Half-hardy, suitable for drying; any soil, sun	15-30cm (6-12in)	Summer-autumn
	Helichrysum bracteatum vars.	Half-hardy, everlastings; light soil, sun	30-90cm (1-3ft)	Summer-early autumn
	Hibiscus trionum vars.	Hardy, short-lived blooms; rich moist soil, sun	60-120cm (2-4ft)	Late summer
	Iberis amara	Hardy; easy, good for cutting; any soil, sun	38cm (15in)	Summer-autumn

	NAME	DESCRIPTION/SITE	HEIGHT	SEASON
ANNUALS (cont)	*Linaria maroccana*	Hardy, snapdragon-like; any soil, sun	23-60cm (9-24in)	Summer
	Linum grandiflorum	Hardy and easy; well-drained soil, sun	30-45cm (1-1½ft)	Summer
	Malcolmia maritima	Hardy, fragrant; well-drained soil, sun	20cm (8in)	Spring-autumn
	Matthiola incana vars.	Hardy, richly scented; good soil, sun/light shade	30-75cm (1-2½ft)	Summer
	Mimulus cupreus vars.	Half-hardy, compact; moist soil, shade	15-30cm (6-12in)	Summer-autumn
	Papaver rhoeas	Hardy, seed pods; any, even poor soil, sun	60cm (2ft)	Summer
	P. somniferum	Hardy, blue-green leaves, seed pods; any soil, sun	75cm (2½ft)	Late spring
	Salvia splendens	Half-hardy, bedding plants; well-drained soil, sun	60-90cm (2-3ft)	Summer-autumn
	Schizanthus pinnatus	Half-hardy, fern-like foliage; moist soil, sun/shelter	30-45cm (1-1½ft)	Summer-autumn
BORDER PLANTS	*Aethionema pulchellum*	Evergreen sub-shrub; well-drained soil, sun	15-23cm (6-9in)	Late spring-summer
	Allium roseum	Bulbous, long-lasting; well-drained soil, sun	30cm (1ft)	Early summer
	Amaryllis belladonna	Half-hardy bulb; sandy loam, sun and shelter	60-75cm (2-2½ft)	Autumn
	Anemone x *hybrida* vars.	Tough once established; moist soil, sun, shade	0.9-1.5m (3-5ft)	Late summer-autumn
	Armeria maritima	Evergreen, clump-forming; well-drained soil, sun	30cm (1ft)	Spring-summer
	Astilbe sp. and vars.	Attractive foliage; moist to wet soil, sun/shade	45cm-1.2m (1½ft-4ft)	Summer
	Bergenia sp. and vars.	Evergreen, leathery leaves; any soil, shade/sun	30-38cm (12-15in)	Early-late spring
	Centaurea dealbata	Deeply cut, hairy leaves; any soil, sun	60cm (2ft)	Early summer-autumn
	Centranthus ruber	Extremely hardy and self-seeding; limy soil, sun	45-90cm (1½-3ft)	Summer
	Dierama pulcherrimum	Grass-like foliage; well-drained rich soil, sun and shelter	0.9-1.8m (3-6ft)	Late summer-autumn
	Digitalis x *mertonensis*	Evergreen, tapering spikes; moist soil, light shade	60-90cm (2-3ft)	Summer-early autumn
	Erythronium dens-canis	Brown-blotched leaves, moist rich soil, shade	10-15cm (4-6in)	Spring
	Eupatorium purpureum	Suitable for semi-wild areas; moist soil, sun/shade	0.6-1.8m (2-6ft)	Summer-autumn
	Euphorbia griffithii 'Fireglow'	Herbaceous, colourful bracts; any soil, sun	75cm (2½ft)	Late spring
	Filipendula purpurea	Hand-shaped foliage; any soil, sun/light shade	90cm (3ft)	Summer
	Geum x *borisii*	Clump-forming evergreen; good soil, sun/light shade	30cm (1ft)	Summer-autumn
	Helleborus orientalis	Handsome, near evergreen foliage; deep moist soil, shade	60cm (2ft)	Winter-spring
	Heuchera sanguinea	Hairy leaf mats; light soil, sun/light shade	60cm (2ft)	Summer-autumn
	Incarvillea delavayi	Handsome lobed leaves; rich soil, sun	60cm (2ft)	Spring-early summer
	Kniphofia vars.	Specimen plants; any well-drained soil, sun	0.6-1.8m (2-6ft)	Summer-autumn
	Lamium maculatum	Excellent ground cover; any soil, sun or shade	30cm (1ft)	Spring-autumn
	Liatris spicata	Grassy leaf clumps; moist soil, sun	90cm (3ft)	Late summer
	Lobelia sp. and vars.	Handsome foliage; rich moist soil, light shade	0.75-1.2m (2½-4ft)	Summer-autumn
	Lychnis sp.	Often silvery foliage; any soil, sun/light shade	to 90cm (3ft)	Spring-late summer
	Lythrum salicaria, L. virgatum	Suitable as waterside plants; moist soil, sun	0.6-1.5m (2-5ft)	Summer-autumn
	Malva alcae	Ultra-hardy; any soil, light shade	0.6-1.2m (2-4ft)	Summer-autumn
	Nerine bowdenii	Bulbous, near-hardy; well-drained soil, sun/wall shelter	40-60cm (16-24in)	Autumn
	Paeonia lactiflora vars.	Long-lived, handsome leaves; rich well-drained soil, sun/light shade	0.75-1m (2½-3ft)	Early summer
	Papaver orientale vars.	Ultra-hardy, floppy habit, hairy; any, poor soil, sun	60-90cm (2-3ft)	Early summer
	Penstemon sp. and vars.	Border and rock plants; any soil, sun	10-90cm (4-36in)	Summer-autumn
	Phlox paniculata vars.	Long-lived; fertile soil, sun/light shade	to 1m (40in)	Summer-autumn
	Physostegia virginianum	Ultra-hardy, trouble-free; any soil, sun/shade	50cm (26in)	Summer
	Pyrethrum roseum vars.	Feathery foliage; light soil, sun	75-90cm (2½-3ft)	Summer
	Salvia fulgens	Near-hardy; well-drained rich soil, sun	90cm (3ft)	Summer-autumn
	Saponaria ocymoides	Vigorous and compact; any soil, sun/light shade	15cm (6in)	Spring-autumn
	Schizostylis coccinea	Near-hardy bulb; moist soil, sun and shelter	60-90cm (2-3ft)	Autumn
	Stokesia laevis	Easy and ultra-hardy; light soil, sun/shade	30-45cm (1-1½ft)	Summer-autumn
	Thymus sp. and vars.	Evergreen creeping mats; any soil, sun	2.5-30cm (1-12in)	Late spring-summer
	Zauschneria californica	Near-hardy, grassy foliage; light soil, sun and shelter	30-45cm (1-1½ft)	Summer-autumn

Blue and mauve flowers

Echoing the colour of the sky, blue flowers have many shades. They vary from the cool and crisp colours of a spring morning to the misty grey-blues of autumn, and from the near purple of gathering dusk to rich midnight blue. Some popular border plants, such as irises and delphiniums, cover all these colour ranges while others have such distinctive tones that they have become part of our descriptive language – think of forget-me-not and cornflower blue.

There are few true blue flowers. The majority incline either to cool white-blue shades or dark and intense mauves and purple-reds. And in spite of many attempts and much cross-breeding, there are no blue roses or tulips; but the hybrid tea rose 'Blue Moon' or the 'Blue Parrot' tulip can be successfully incorporated in all-blue planting schemes. Luckily, blue flowers rarely clash with one another – although some of the most beautiful, like the gentians and the Himalayan blue poppies (*Meconopsis* species), have exacting growing demands that exclude them from certain soils and sites.

Clear blues – campanulas and agapanthus, for example – look cool and tranquil and, like pale blue, are most effective in dark settings. Picture bluebells in dappled woodland light or *Rhododendron augustinii* against its own glossy dark green foliage. Dark blues make little impact from a distance, although they can be exquisite close to, or in pale surroundings. Rich blue monkshoods (*Aconitum*) contrast magnificently with golden-leaved spiraeas or elder (*Sambucus racemosa* 'Plumosa Aurea'). Violet and purple shades – in asters, lilacs, violas and pansies – can introduce warmth and contrast to potentially sugary pale blues.

Shades of blue Deep blue delphiniums vie with purple verbascums and lilac campanulas.

COOL AND DISTANT BLUES

**Associations of all blue flowers evoke a
cool relaxed mood – and help to increase the apparent
size of a small garden.**

Blue flowers cover a wide range of qualities from cold, even frosty tints to the deeper, warmer, more purple shades that carry a hint of red. Such variety means that blues mix happily with most other colours – and they also make successful associations in themselves. The range of shades and tints creates interest, yet because the flowers are one basic colour they make for harmonious grouping.

As you create your blue partnerships, bear in mind the following points. Light blues, surrounded by grey or silver foliage, become more luminous, making them excellent subjects for planting in beds around a patio where you sit or entertain in the evening. Blues with a touch of red will be less luminous, but they can be used to add warmth to groupings dominated by cool blues.

All blues, but especially the paler tints, are recessive – they draw the eye after them. This makes them invaluable for giving the impression of extra depth. Placed at the end of a small plot, the misty blues of forget-me-nots, catmint, delphiniums, caryopteris and some of the Michaelmas daisies make the garden look longer than it really is.

The use of a single colour means that the form, texture and overall habit of the plants should be considered carefully to avoid monotony. A successful grouping of blue-flowered bulbs in spring could include the spiked flowerheads of grape hyacinths (*Muscari armeniacum*), the delicate star-shaped *Chionodoxa* and blue forms of the daisy-like *Anemone blanda*.

In a sunny herbaceous border in summer plenty of contrast would be provided by the pincushion-like flowerheads of *Scabiosa caucasica* growing alongside *Linum narbonense* (which has sparkling funnel-like blooms). Then add the saucer-shaped flowers of *Veronica incana* or *Veronica spicata*.

▶ **Partners for a rose** In early summer, the shrub rose 'Nevada' becomes a fountain of gorgeous blooms whose white crispness is perfectly partnered by spires of blue delphiniums and delicate bells of *Campanula persicifolia*. In the foreground, a clump of spiderwort (*Tradescantia* × *andersoniana*) continues the blue theme to ground level.

135

▲ **Rock garden in spring** A lightly shaded rock garden is the ideal site for the little squill (*Scilla sibirica*). Violet cress (*Ionopsidium acaule*) would be a suitable companion; it is a diminutive annual, only 5cm (2in) high, that can be sown in autumn to provide a close, lilac-tinted carpet the following spring.

▲ **Harmony in lilac** Irises and lupins make perfect partners for all-blue associations in the summer border. The pale lilac-blue blooms of the bearded iris 'Jane Phillips' lend emphasis to the contrasting shape and colour of the elegant spikes of darker Russell lupins. Similar contrast is found in the foliage, where the stiff blue-green sword-shaped leaves of the iris support the floppy, sage-green lupin foliage.

◄ **Carpet of blue** The evergreen sweetly scented *Daphne odora* 'Aureomarginata' has a somewhat sprawling habit. Its appearance is improved with a carpet of blue spring flowers. Try dark blue *Viola labradorica* 'Purpurea' with the clear daisy flowers of *Anemone blanda*, the club-shaped heads of pale blue *Muscari armeniacum* and, at the back, a cloud of Spanish bluebells (*Endymion hispanicus*).

▲ Clothing a wall in colour This outstanding group planting is all the more eye-catching for the imaginative use of contrasting flower shapes and shades. The deciduous ceanothus which, in the shelter of the sunny wall, flowers for most of the summer, is laden with fluffy panicles of misty blue that offset the nodding sky-blue flowers of its climbing partner, *Clematis* 'Perle d'Azur'.

Below, revelling in the warmth of the site, a clump of agapanthus raises huge rounded heads of violet-blue flowers.

► Cornflower blue A charming mixture of cottage-garden annuals is dominated by the round flower heads of rich blue cornflowers (*Centaurea cyanus*) that bloom throughout summer and into early autumn. The annual lupins (*Lupinus nanus*), with dainty spikes in white, blue and pink, flower for as many months, long after their perennial relatives have given up.

▲ **Frosty-white blues** The spring-flowering *Puschkinia scilloides* is also known as striped squill from the icy-blue stripes on its white, hyacinth-like clusters. It blends well with the purple foliage and flowers of the pansy *Viola labradorica* 'Purpurea'.

▶ **Purple warmth** Purple-blue spikes of *Salvia* × *superba* introduce a hint of warmth to tall, cool blue delphiniums.

▼ **Summer cool** Palest blue campanulas and white-eyed delphiniums mixed with white lavateras create a pool of refreshing calm in the heat of summer.

BLUE AND YELLOW

Plant groupings of complementary blues and yellows to give character and individuality to the smallest garden.

Blue is a popular colour with many people, but the paler tones can appear frosty and hard unless they are livened up with touches of warmer colours. Equally, the hot shades of violet and mauve can seem dull and lost in their own shadows unless bright flowers enclose them within a small space. In both of these instances yellow flowers are the perfect companions, warming cool blue tints and bringing dark shades into sharp relief.

Colour harmony is a basic element in good garden design, but successful associations are not achieved by simply mixing two colour ranges. Harmony – or contrast – in shape and texture is just as important. Avoid mixing too many daisy flowers or spikes or fluffy panicles, but include contrasting shapes, such as slender spires of lavender-blue catmint (*Nepeta × faassenii*) with the yellow or orange daisy flowers of pot marigolds (*Calendula officinalis*); or try pale blue, club-shaped grape hyacinths (*Muscari armeniacum* 'Cantab') against the pale yellow primroses of *Primula vulgaris*.

Spring and summer partners

Blue and yellow are natural spring partners: forget-me-nots with pale yellow tulips or golden-orange wallflowers; porcelain-blue chionodoxas with yellow *Alyssum saxatile*, or, by the poolside, slender blue Jacob's ladder (*Polemonium caeruleum*) above the glistening gold of double-flowered marsh marigolds (*Caltha palustris* 'Flore Pleno').

In summer, cool associations of blue and yellow calm senses satiated with vibrant colours. Blue irises or delphiniums can be partnered with yellow shrub roses, and formal beds of the hybrid tea rose 'Spek's Yellow' look even more luminous within a front edge of clear blue *Geranium* 'Johnson's Blue'. The pale blue *Clematis* 'Mrs Cholmondely' looks magnificent against a wall in the company of the yellow climbing

rose 'Mermaid'. Impressive focal points can be created in the herbaceous border with clumps of sky-blue Himalayan poppies (*Meconopsis betonicifolia*) rising from a footing of golden-leaved *Hosta fortunei* 'Albopicta'.

Blue is scarce in autumn, apart from Michaelmas daisies and the blue flowers of *Aster novi-belgii* 'Professor Kippenburg', set against yellow-green *Kniphofia* 'Percy's Pride'.

▼ **Summer peace** Set against yellow meadow rue (*Thalictrum speciosissimum*), delphiniums and bellflowers create an oasis of calm with madonna lilies (*Lilium candidum*) and *Nicotiana alata* 'Lime Green'.

► **Asters to the fore** Amellus asters can be a better choice than the related Michaelmas daisies, since they are both long-lived and trouble-free. A hybrid from that species, *A.* × *frikartii*, fills the late-summer border with daisy-flowered blooms for several months. Lavender-blue in the variety 'Mönch', it is shadowed here by the towering stems of the 1.2m (4ft) tall *Oenothera lamarckiana* set with golden-yellow flower funnels.

▼ **Heavenly blue** From early summer until early autumn the prostrate alpine *Lithospermum diffusum* 'Heavenly Blue', now known as *Lithodora diffusa*, spreads shrubby mats over the rock garden, almost hidden by a profusion of deep blue, funnel-shaped flowers. They are beautifully set off by the golden-yellow clusters of *Genista lydia* and the young, gold-tipped shoots of a dwarf spruce (*Abies*). In the foreground, a buckler fern (*Dryopteris villarii*) raises its sage-green fronds in a sea of blue.

► **Summer beds** The hardy annual *Convolvulus tricolor* has all of the advantages and none of the problems associated with its close relative, the pernicious bindweed. The variety 'Blue Flash' forms compact plants, about 23cm (9in) high, of brilliant blue flowers, the centres marked with white and yellow stars. It blooms from summer until early autumn, in happy association with the floppy, golden-yellow Californian poppies (*Eschscholzia californica*) guarded by tall-stemmed white-flowered *Penstemon* × *gloxiniodes*.

◄ **Winter joy** Unscathed by snow and frost, the small bulbous *Iris histrioides* 'Major' raises its royal blue flowers in mid winter. It is distinguished by a narrow orange ridge on the lower falls of the blooms, echoed in the orange stamens of the February-flowering *Crocus chrysanthus*. Both will thrive in light, dappled shade but show off their intense colours best in full sun.

▲ Blue and yellow duet The satiny blue flowers of *Geranium ibericum*, with mounds of deeply lobed leaves, nestle at the feet of 90cm (3ft) tall *Phlomis russeliana* set with tiers of creamy-yellow tubular flowers.

▼ Easter joy The little pasque flower (*Pulsatilla vulgaris*) opens its downy buds to purple, golden-centred cups in late spring. At the same time, the 15cm (6in) high *Tulipa tarda* spreads its yellow petals into wide stars.

▲ Summer tapestry *Salvia patens*, a half-hardy annual, weaves its clear blue flowers through equally tender primrose-yellow *Chrysanthemum frutescens*. The daisy-flower shape is repeated in golden gazanias.

BLUE AND ORANGE

Create eye-catching groups from drifts of blue flowers that complement and soften vivid orange flowers.

Complementary colours enliven one another and few combinations are as powerful as blue and orange. Use such bold mixtures carefully to create schemes that will give welcome contrast to the more subtle colour associations likely to dominate the garden.

The brilliance of such contrasts can be toned down by using a lighter tint of one colour with a darker shade of the other. In spring, pale forget-me-nots make a misty blue carpet for startling orange tulips, such as 'Orange Bouquet', or orange wallflowers, such as 'Allegretto'. This group could be planted at the front of a mixed border and later replaced by summer bedding. For an enchanting display on a similar colour theme, grow petunia 'Resisto Blue' with the hot-orange French marigold 'Paprika'.

Blue and orange combinations look especially effective when chosen to contrast different growth habits. The dense 25cm (10in) tufts of the graceful, blue-grey perennial grass *Festuca glauca* make handsome partners in front of the shrubby potentilla 'Tangerine' whose coppery-orange flowers appear continuously from early summer to early autumn.

You could edge a border with the little tufted pansy, *Viola cornuta* 'Belmont Blue', whose pale sky-blue flowers look glorious below the Welsh poppy (*Meconopsis cambrica*). Flowering the whole summer and well into autumn, this grows to a height of about 45cm (1½ft) and though usually yellow also comes in orange shades.

On a sunny wall, the saucer-shaped blooms of blue morning glory (*Ipomoea tricolor*) could combine exquisitely with the orange of the Chilean glory flower (*Eccremocarpus scaber*).

▶ **Colour contrasts** The large, purplish-blue flowers of *Clematis* 'Lasurstern' stand out strikingly against the slender clusters of orange-yellow honeysuckle (*Lonicera × tellmanniana*) that decorate a wall in early summer.

▶ **Good companions**
The impressive bulbous plant *Camassia leichtlinii* raises 90cm (3ft) tall spikes of starry flowers above tufts of grassy foliage in early summer. Their pale blue tones temper the vivid orange of a front planting of Siberian wallflowers (*Cheiranthus × allionii*).

▲ **Late-summer brilliance**
Planted in a sunny sheltered spot,
Agapanthus 'Headbourne Hybrids' put
on a massed display of vivid blue in late
summer. The rounded flower heads
contrast effectively with the taller spikes
of orange-red *Curtonus paniculatus*, a
montbretia-like perennial.

◄ **Blue streak** Spikes of palest blue
delphinium add vertical interest to a
dense planting of globe flowers and
soften their colourful impact. Happiest
in moist soil, the globe flower (*Trollius
chinensis* 'Imperial Orange') unfolds its
brilliant orange-yellow blooms in late
spring and early summer.

► **Cascades of blue** In late May,
the evergreen ceanothus hybrid, *C.* ×
'Cascade' becomes a shimmering
waterfall of rich blue flower panicles. At
its feet ripple the last waves of orange-
coloured wallflowers (*Cheiranthus* ×
allionii).

▲ **A gift from the hills** The intense blue flowers of hound's tongue (*Cynoglossum nervosum*) resemble forget-me-nots, although they are borne on much taller, hairy-leaved plants that originate in the Himalayas. Flowering in mid summer, it associates well with the arching orange-red flower spikes of *Crocosmia × crocosmiiflora*.

◄ **Summer splendour** The purple-blue flowers of the shrubby *Salvia officinalis* 'Purpurascens' lose their dominance in the company of the modern shrub rose 'Graham Thomas', fragrant and apricot-yellow in bud, opening to clear yellow.

▼ **Spring bedding** The blue-faced pansy *Viola* 'Crystal Bowl Blue' spreads an exquisite carpet for the stout 60cm (2ft) tall stems of the Triumph tulip 'Dutch Princess', whose glowing orange goblets open in April and May.

BLUE AND RED

Create vivid colour splashes in herbaceous borders and temper their impact with silvery and grey foliage plants.

Strong blues and vivid reds make for powerful, even aggressive associations. They should always be used with discretion and in small doses, rather like exclamation marks in borders otherwise dominated by pastel colours.

Blue and red partnerships are most common in the summer garden, apart from such classic late-spring schemes as Spanish bluebells (*Endymion hispanicus*) with red polyanthus primroses, and forget-me-nots or grape hyacinths (*Muscari armeniacum*) carpeting red or pink tulips.

Traditionally, roses of all types and colours are married with blue delphiniums, lavender, pansies or catmint (*Nepeta* × *faassenii*), and many climbing red roses share the wall space with large-flowered blue Jackmanii clematis.

In general, it is advisable to mix strong blue flowers with deep pink and clear cerise rather than bright scarlet. Alternatively, use misty blue or lavender tones to partner crimson and purple-red shades. It is, though, possible to position two strong colours near each other as long as they are separated by foliage plants that harmonize with both. Silvery plants such as *Stachys lanata*, wormwood (*Artemisia absinthium*) and *Senecio maritimus* 'Silver Dust' are particularly effective as foils among brilliantly coloured blooms.

Tender bedding fuchsias are so exquisite in bloom that they demand companions that will complement rather than compete with their beauty. You could underplant container-grown fuchsias like the red and purple 'Mrs Popple' with pale blue annual *Lobelia erinus* 'Cambridge Blue' or, in the mixed border, edge it with the clear blue cups of *Campanula carpatica*.

The lavender-blue bells of *Campanula lactiflora* are indispensable in any summer border; they look magnificent in association with almost all other flowers and in particular with the foxglove-like spires of penstemons. Try siting them next to varieties of *Penstemon campanulatus*, such as the scarlet 'Firebird' or the salmon-red 'King George'.

On a sheltered and sunny wall dressed with the splendid purple-blue climbing *Solanum crispum*, in bloom from June right through until autumn, a footing of clear pink petunias would make a perfect companion.

◄ **Autumn brilliance** The silver-white, woolly foliage of *Artemisia ludoviciana* separates two vivid colours in this early-autumn scene. At the back are the clear pink daisy flowers of *Aster novae-angliae* 'Harrington's Pink', the colour complemented by the carmine-pink flower domes of *Sedum spectabile* 'Carmen' at the front. Effective contrast in colour and form is provided by agapanthus whose bright blue flower umbels rise above clumps of glossy green leaves.

▲ **Spring carpets** Grape hyacinths (*Muscari armeniacum*) spread readily to form a carpet of cobalt-blue. It is punctuated with perfect reddish-purple globes of the drumstick primrose (*Primula denticulata*).

► **Summer brightness** Violet-blue *Geranium ibericum* remains in bloom long after peonies have enjoyed their brilliant but brief display.

▼ **Rose companions** Catmint (*Nepeta × faassenii*) flowers through summer and autumn. It is an ideal edging plant for roses, as here, where it fronts the clear pink shrub rose 'Constance Spry'.

LAVENDER AND MAUVE

**For pretty plant associations use the
subtle range of mauves to bridge the gap between
tints of blue, violet and pinky red.**

Mauve is one of the more gentle colours in the garden. Soft and misty, it ranges from pinky blue to the paler shades of purple. Choose from the wide range of mauve flowers to complement pink, pinkish blue and purple-flowering plants, perhaps combined with grey and silver foliage.

Such harmonious associations would look elegant in a window-box or in containers on a patio. For long-lasting effect, try mauve, pink and blue petunias complemented by the silvery leaves of *Senecio maritimus*.

For colour contrast with mauve, especially its deeper, bluer shades, choose the paler yellow flowers, such as the yellowish greens of foaming lady's mantle (*Alchemilla mollis*) or angelica (*Angelica archangelica*) with its rounded flower heads.

In mid and late spring, sulphur yellow *Alyssum saxatile* 'Citrinum' is a better partner for mauve aubrietas than the bright yellow of its normal form, creating a calmer association for rock gardens and retaining walls.

Several rhododendrons have mauve flowers, including the popular *Rhododendron ponticum* – a useful evergreen screen. For a partnership with long-lasting interest, plant evergreen *Helleborus lividus corsicus* and *Corydalis lutea* in the foreground: the hellebore's cup-shaped, apple-green flowers open from early spring, before the rhododendron's, but remain beautiful for a long time, while the corydalis produces a mass of tubular yellow flowers from mid spring until autumn.

The small hooded flowers of catmint (*Nepeta* × *faassenii*), in a misty shade of mauve with more than a touch of blue, are set off to perfection by its grey-green foliage. In early to mid summer they look charming with *Erigeron* × *hybridus* whose many-petalled, daisy-like blooms provide a contrast of flower form in harmonizing shades of pink and mauve-pink. For a quiet background, plant the grey, finely divided leaves of the 90cm (3ft) tall wormwood (*Artemisia absinthium* 'Lambrook Silver'). Alternatively, for a contrast in colour and flower form, plant a clump of pale yellow day lilies with large upward-facing trumpet-shaped flowers. At the rear, imposing delphiniums in mauves and pinks could add vertical interest.

Acanthus spinosus – bear's breeches – carries its mauve and white hooded flowers in mid and late summer on long-lasting statuesque spikes up to 1.5m (5ft) tall. The beautiful deeply divided leaves are best partnered with plants that have contrasting foliage forms but flowers that harmonize with the *Acanthus*. For example, the purple, rather rounded and fleshy leaves of the 60cm (2ft) tall *Sedum maximum* 'Atropurpureum', with similarly coloured flower heads, is a suitable foreground partner. Alongside the *Acanthus*, plant *Aster* × *frikartii* 'Mönch' with soft lavender-blue, yellow-centred daisies lasting until early autumn. Behind, to complete the group, could be planted the tree mallow (*Lavatera olbia*) which bears its purple-pink, hollyhock-like flowers until the early frosts.

◄ **Shades of purple** The stately foxglove (*Digitalis purpurea*) makes a stunning impression in summer with its tall spikes rising above hairy leaves. The 'Excelsior' strain includes white, pink and mauve flowers, worthy companions for the dark *Rosa rugosa* 'Roseraie de l'Hay'. The colour theme is strengthened by a front planting of magenta *Geranium psilostemon* and frothy pink bells of *Heuchera sanguinea* 'Scintillation'.

◄ Elegant mauves The Californian annual *Clarkia elegans* covers a wide colour range, from pink and scarlet, orange and white to lavender and purple. It blooms nonstop from mid summer until early autumn; here its colourful, 45cm (1½ft) tall spikes of flowers draw the eye upwards from the foliage of two plants which have finished flowering, irises and Oriental poppies.

▼ Summer pastels The clear mauve lace-caps of *Hydrangea villosa* are in perfect harmony with the crisp pink clusters of *Phlox paniculata*. A background of the purple-leaved *Berberis thunbergii* 'Rose Glow' perfectly highlights the pastel colours at the front.

▲ **Winter tapestry** The evergreen heath (*Erica carnea*) is one of our most popular winter-flowering plants. It forms wide hummocks of attractive ground cover and from late autumn until well into spring blossoms with neat sprays of white, pink, red, purple and mauve flowers.

Here, the deep pinkish-mauve 'Winter Beauty' is pierced in spring by the dainty stems and glossy strap-like leaves of the aptly named glory-in-the-snow (*Chionodoxa luciliae*). Its porcelain-blue, white-centred flowers gleam like jewels among the flowers and leaves of the heather.

▼ **Summer abundance** A bold blend of pale and deeper mauve erupts in sheer exuberance on this garden wall in early summer. Two clematis hybrids entwine each other, giving mutual support, neither overpowering the other but creating a picture of perfect harmony.

In the foreground, the delicate sprays of meadow rue (*Thalictrum delavayi*) repeat the colour association while its ferny foliage adds a delicate footnote. On a practical level, the foliage also provides the necessary shade over the shallow clematis roots, which must be protected from strong sun.

◄ **Colour in the shade** The Lenten rose (*Helleborus orientalis*) first opens its nodding flower cups in late winter and goes on well into spring. Extremely variable in colour, the flowers may be cream or white, pink or plum-coloured but are always heavily flecked with crimson-purple inside as if to show off the golden-yellow stamens. Shade-loving, Lenten roses are ideal for the front of shrub borders, accompanied in early spring by small pink-flowered *Primula vulgaris*, and after flowering suppressing weeds with their evergreen, leathery leaves.

▼ **Blaze that unfolds** With its grassy foliage and dense flower spikes, blazing star or gayfeather (*Liatris spicata*) resembles a small red-hot poker. In contrast, though, liatris opens its flowers from the top down until the spike is a living flame of vibrant colour in the late-summer border. Against this dramatic purple-pink background a stand of clear pink antirrhinums seems to become almost translucent.

BLUE THROUGH THE YEAR

**Cool blues and rich mauves follow the
progress of the seasons, echoing the changing
sky and the intensity of daylight.**

Blue is the colour of the little cheerful bulbs that greet the spring – purple blue crocus and clear blue muscaris, scillas and hyacinths. They are joined by the pretty, cup-shaped *Anemone apennina* and *A. blanda* and, in shady rock gardens, by *Hepatica nobilis* that is often mistaken for the anemone.

There are purple-blue rhododendrons (*R. augustinia* and *R. ponticum*) and the magnificent Kurume azaleas. One broom, *Cytisus purpureus*, departs from the usual yellow flowers of the species to wreathe its wand-like stems in purple pea-like blooms in late spring.

Most blue flowers, though, belong in the summer garden. Few borders are without such ever popular plants as delphiniums, bell-flowered campanulas, irises, sweet peas, lupins and scabious. The vivid blue gentians can be difficult to grow, but they are so exquisite in form and colour that they are worth cosseting. The spring-flowering *Gentian acaulis* is a lot easier than the star-like *G. verna* that demands limy soil to thrive. *G. septemfida*, which in spite of its name flowers in mid and late summer, is the easiest of all, bearing clusters of deep blue trumpet-like flowers.

As summer merges into autumn, the blues become deeper. Pale blue summer-flowering ceanothus gives way to the rich blue panicles of the evergreen *C.* × *burkwoodii* and the ultra hardy *C.* 'Autumnal Blue'. *Buddleia davidii*, beloved by butterflies, is deep purple in 'Black Knight', and purple-blue is also the colour of *Clematis heracleifolia*. This is not the usual climbing clematis but a true herbaceous perennial that in early autumn bears tubular flowers on 90cm (3ft) tall stems.

Winter blues in the garden are confined to the brave pansies and the brilliantly blue little *Iris histrioides* and *I. reticulata*.

▼ **Perennial blues** Large-flowered delphinium hybrids come in all shades of blue, clearer and brighter than the nearby sprays of *Anchusa azurea*. Pink lupins complete the picture.

▶ **Summer exotics** At the height of summer, the graceful umbels of violet-blue *Agapanthus* 'Headbourne Hybrids' unfold above clumps of narrow strap-shaped leaves. They contrast in shape with the slender stems of exotic-looking Cape figwort (*Phygelius capensis*) tinkling with scarlet, tubular flowers, and with the deeply cut foliage of the tree peony (*Paeonia lutea ludlowii*) in the background.

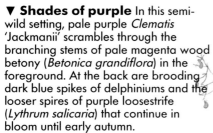

▼ **Shades of purple** In this semi-wild setting, pale purple *Clematis* 'Jackmanii' scrambles through the branching stems of pale magenta wood betony (*Betonica grandiflora*) in the foreground. At the back are brooding dark blue spikes of delphiniums and the looser spires of purple loosestrife (*Lythrum salicaria*) that continue in bloom until early autumn.

▲ **Summer clouds** Airy lilac-blue wands of catmint (*Nepeta × faassenii*) are a perfect foil for the pale yellow trumpets of fleeting day lilies (*Hemerocallis* hybrids). Both are hardy border perennials that increase steadily over the years. The catmint flowers throughout summer and autumn, long after the day lilies have died back to grassy foliage clumps.

◄ **Autumn blues** In late summer and early autumn, Russian sage (*Perovskia atriplicifolia*) decks its downy, grey-white stems with a mass of small violet-blue flowers. Their tubular shape is repeated in the clear pink spikes of *Penstemon × gloxinioides*.

▶ **Autumn fruits** The evergreen shrub *Berberis darwinii*, named in honour of Charles Darwin, is a year-long delight. In spring the glossy, holly-like leaves are hidden behind showers of brilliant orange-yellow blooms, and by autumn the branches are weighed down with clusters of blue-black, grape-bloomed fruit. At a height and spread of 2.4m (8ft), it makes an outstanding contribution to the shrub border and is also suitable as a hedging plant.

▼ **Autumn sunshine** From late summer on, pride of place in the herbaceous border goes to the Michaelmas daisies (*Aster novi-belgii*) whose splendid daisy flowers come in colour ranges that span every shade of blue, pink and purple. They are frequently partnered by perennial sunflowers (*Helianthus decapetalus*) whose golden blooms glow in the autumn sunshine.

▶ **September colour** Few shrubs flower in the autumn garden and rarely in the unique shade of purple-blue. *Hydrangea villosa* is one exception, its large flat lace-caps gleaming against the velvety leaves when it is given the lightly shaded position it prefers. The purple theme is picked up and repeated in the hydrangea's close companions, a dwarf sand cherry (*Prunus* × *cistena*) on one side and the purple-pink of *Anemone* × *hybrida* 'Mont Rose' on the other. Bright gold is supplied by a sprawling group of St John's wort (*Hypericum* 'Hidcote'), at the foot of the taller plants.

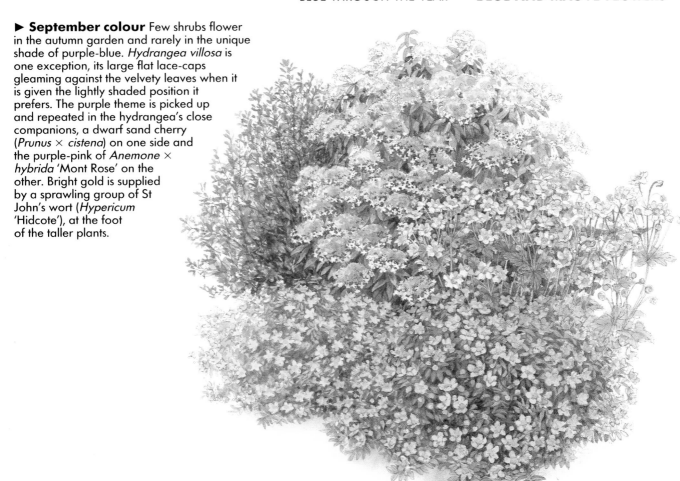

◀ **Winter miniatures** As early as January the slender buds of *Crocus tomasinianus* push through the ground and at the merest touch of sun open their pale lilac goblets to show off the golden stamens inside. They naturalize easily among other late-winter bulbs, such as golden aconites (*Eranthis hyemalis*) and hardy cyclamens like *Cyclamen hederifolium* whose autumn flowers have given way to a carpet of handsome marbled leaves.

► **Shady rock gardens** A north or east-facing rock garden is the favoured site for many spring-flowering alpines, notably the anemone-like *Hepatica nobilis* whose lavender-blue flowers seem flecked with gold dust. Primula hybrids (*P.* × *pubescens*) revel in similar conditions, their dense heads of mauve and purple beautifully contrasting with the silver marbled leaves of *Cyclamen neapolitanum.*

◄ **Spring bedding** The hardy hybrids of *Hyacinthus orientalis* include white and yellow, pink and red, and blue and purple named varieties. The deep purple-blue 'Ostara' creates a stunning carpet in late spring, embroidered here and there with the red splashes of the tiny bedding daisy, *Bellis perennis* 'Red Carpet'.

BLUE AND MAUVE COLOURED FLOWERS

	NAME	DESCRIPTION/SITE	HEIGHT	SEASON
SHRUBS	Abutilon vitifolium	Near-hardy evergreen; well-drained soil, sun and shelter	2.4m (8ft)	Late spring-autumn
	Buddleia alternifolia, B. davidii, B. fallowiana	Deciduous, weeping habit; loamy soil, sun	2.7-6m (9-20ft)	Early summer-autumn
	Callicarpa bodinieri giraldii	Deciduous, autumn tints; rich soil, sun/shelter	1.8-2.4m (6-8ft)	Summer
	Calluna vulgaris 'Silver Queen'	Evergreen, silvery foliage; lime-free soil, sun	25-30cm (10-12in)	Summer-autumn
	Caryopteris x clandonensis	Deciduous, grey-green foliage; any soil, sun	0.6-1.2m (2-4ft)	Summer-autumn
	Ceanothus sp. and vars.	Deciduous and evergreen; light soil, sun and shelter	1.8-6m (6-20ft)	Spring-autumn
	Ceratostigma plumbaginoides	Deciduous, half-hardy; loamy soil, sun/shelter	30cm (1ft)	Summer-autumn
	Clematis alpina, C. macropetala	Deciduous climbers; well-drained soil incl. limy, sun, roots in shade	1.8-3.6m (6-12ft)	Late spring-early summer
	Cytisus purpureus	Deciduous, spreading; any or poor soil, sun	30-60cm (1-2ft)	Late spring-summer
	Daphne odora	Evergreen, glossy foliage; well-drained soil, sun, wall shelter	1.5-1.8m (5-6ft)	Winter-spring
	Fuchsia 'Dr Foster'	Deciduous, bushy; loamy soil, sun/light shade	to 1.2m (4ft)	Summer-autumn
	Hebe sp. and vars.	Near-hardy evergreen, grey foliage; any soil/sun	15cm-1.8m (6in-6ft)	Late spring-autumn
	Hibiscus syriacus vars.	Deciduous, upright; good well-drained soil, sun/shelter	1.8-3m (6-10ft)	Summer-autumn
	Hydrangea macrophylla, H. serrata vars.	Deciduous, rounded habit; moist soil, light shade/shelter	0.9-1.5m (3-5ft)	Late summer-autumn
	Lavandula sp. and vars.	Evergreen, grey-green foliage; any soil, sun	30cm-1.2m (1-4ft)	Summer-autumn
	Passiflora caerulea	Semi-hardy evergreen climber; well-drained soil, sun/shelter	6m (20ft)	Summer-early autumn
	Perovskia atriplicifolia	Deciduous, excellent for coastal regions; light soil, sun	0.9-1.5m (3-5ft)	Summer-autumn
	Pittosporum tenuifolium	Semi-hardy evergreen, attractive foliage; good soil, sun and shelter	4.5m (15ft)	Spring
	Rhododendron ponticum vars.	Evergreen, leathery leaves; moist, acid soil, light shade	3.6-6m (12-20ft)	Late spring
	Rosmarinus officinalis	Evergreen, aromatic foliage; light soil, sun	0.9-1.2m (3-4ft)	Summer
	Solanum crispum	Evergreen climber; well-drained soil, sun/shelter	3-6m (10-20ft)	Summer-autumn
	Syringa vulgaris 'Katherine Havemeyer'	Deciduous, strongly fragrant; any soil, sun	2.4-3.6m (8-12ft)	Early summer
	Vinca major, V. minor	Evergreen ground cover; any soil, shade	5-30cm (2-12in)	Spring-autumn
	Wisteria sinensis	Deciduous vigorous climber; deep soil, sun	21m (70ft)	Early summer
ANNUALS AND BIENNIALS	Ageratum houstonianum vars.	Half-hardy, compact; moist soil, sun/shelter	12-30cm (5-12in)	Summer-autumn
	Anagallis arvensis 'Caerulea'	Hardy edging plant; any soil, sun	2.5-5cm (1-2in)	Summer-autumn
	Anchusa capensis	Hardy, compact habit; any soil, sun	23-45cm (9-18in)	Summer
	Callistephus chinensis 'Blue Bedder'	Half-hardy; well-drained soil, sun	15-30cm (6-12in)	Summer-autumn
	Campanula medium	Biennial, self-seeds; any soil, sun/light shade	30-90cm (1-3ft)	Late spring-summer
	Centaurea cyanus vars.	Hardy, easy, good for cutting; any soil, sun	30-90cm (1-3ft)	Summer-autumn
	Cobaea scandens	Half-hardy climber; well-drained soil, sun/shelter	3-6m (10-20ft)	Summer-autumn
	Convolvulus bicolor	Half-hardy, bushy; good soil, sun/shelter	23-38cm (9-15in)	Summer-autumn
	Felicia amelloides	Half-hardy, grey-green leaves; well-drained soil, sun	15-45cm (6-18in)	Summer
	Heliotropium hybrids	Half-hardy, deeply fragrant; fertile soil, sun	45-60cm (1½-2ft)	Summer
	Ipomoea purpurea	Half-hardy vigorous climber; light soil, sun/shelter	2.4-3m (8-10ft)	Summer-autumn
	Lobelia erinus vars.	Half-hardy, compact or trailers; moist soil, sun	10-23cm (4-9in)	Late spring-autumn
	Lupinus nanus 'Pixie Delight'	Hardy, mixed strain; well-drained soil, sun/shade	45cm (1½ft)	Summer-autumn
	Nemophila menziesii	Hardy, compact, suitable for edging; moist soil, sun/light shade	15-23cm (6-9in)	Summer
	Nierembergia repens	Half-hardy, attractive foliage; moist soil, sun	15-20cm (6-8in)	Summer-autumn
	Nigella damascena	Hardy, feathery foliage; any soil, sun	60cm (2ft)	Summer-autumn
	Salvia patens	Half-hardy, upright, branching; any soil, sun	60cm (2ft)	Late summer-autumn

BORDER PLANTS

NAME	DESCRIPTION/SITE	HEIGHT	SEASON
Aconitum carmichaelii, A. napellus	Tough, branching; moist soil, light shade	0.9-1.8m (3-6ft)	Summer-autumn
Allium caeruleum, A. giganteum	Bulbous, attractive seed heads; well-drained soil, sun	0.6-1.5m (2-5ft)	Early summer
Anchusa azurea	Branching, self-seeds; any soil, sun	0.9-1.5cm (3-5ft)	Summer
Anemone blanda, A. coronaria, A. nemorosa	Tuberous, ideal for naturalizing; well-drained soil, sun/light shade	15-30cm (6-12in)	Winter-late spring
Aquilegia bertolonii, A. flabellata	Rock and border plants; moist soil, sun/shade	15-25cm (6-10in)	Late spring-summer
Brunnera macrophylla	Ground-cover plant; any soil, light shade	30-38cm (12-15in)	Late spring-summer
Camassia cusickii, C. esculenta	Bulbous; waterside or border plants, rich moist soil, sun/light shade	60-75cm (2-2½ft)	Summer
Catananche caerulea	Suitable for drying; light soil, sun	45-75cm (1½-2½ft)	Summer
Centaurea montana	Clump-forming, hairy leaves; any soil, sun	60cm (2ft)	Late spring-summer
Chionodoxa sp.	Bulbous, spreads readily; any soil, sun	10-20cm (4-8in)	Spring
Clematis heracleifolia, C. integrifolia	Border plants, fluffy seed heads; alkaline soil, sun/light shade	0.6-1.8m (2-6ft)	Late summer
Colchicum speciosum 'Lilac Wonder'	Suitable for naturalizing; well-drained soil, sun/light shade	15-20cm (6-8in)	Autumn
Cynoglossum nervosum	Hairy foliage; rich soil, sun/light shade	45-60cm (1½-2ft)	Summer
Echinops sp.	Thistle-like leaves, good for drying; any soil, drought-tolerant, sun	0.9-1.5m (3-5ft)	Summer-autumn
Erigeron x hybridus, E. macranthus	Clump-forming, reliable; moist soil, sun	60cm (2ft)	Late spring-summer
Eryngium sp.	Spiny leaves, prickly silver bracts; any soil, sun	30cm-1.2m (1-4ft)	Summer-autumn
Fritillaria meleagris	Bulbous, good for naturalizing; moist soil, shade	25-30cm (10-12in)	Late spring
Galega officinalis	Semi-wild plant; well-drained soil, sun/light shade	0.9-1.5m (3-5ft)	Summer
Gentiana sp.	Herbaceous and evergreen rock and border plants; moist, rich soil, sun/light shade	7.5-60cm (3-24in)	Spring-autumn
Geranium ibericum, G. pratense	Border and edging plants; any soil, sun/light shade	38-60cm (15-24in)	Late spring-summer
Globularia sp.	Evergreen rock garden plants; well-drained soil, sun	2.5-23cm (1-9in)	Late spring-summer
Hepatica nobilis	Rock garden plant; moist soil, shade	7.5-15cm (3-5in)	Late winter-spring
Iris sp. and vars.	Bulbous and rhizomatous; well-drained soil, sun	5cm-1.5m (2in-5ft)	Winter, spring, summer
Limonium latifolium	Clump-forming; any well-drained soil, sun	60cm (2ft)	Summer
Linaria purpurea	Tall spikes, narrow leaves; any soil, sun	1.2m (4ft)	Summer-autumn
Linum narbonense	Free-flowering, narrow foliage; any soil, sun	60cm (2ft)	Summer
Lithospermum sp.	Evergreen carpeters; well-drained soil, sun	10-30cm (4-12in)	Late spring-autumn
Lobelia syphilitica, L. x vedraiensis	Tall flower spikes; rich moist soil, light shade	0.9-1.2m (3-4ft)	Late summer-autumn
Meconopsis betonicifolia	Monocarpic; rich moist soil, semi-shade, shelter	0.9-1.5m (3-5ft)	Summer
Mertensia virginica	Easy-growing, blue-green foliage; rich moist soil, shade	30-60cm (1-2ft)	Late-spring
Muscari armeniacum, M. tubergenianum	Bulbous, strap-shaped leaves; any soil sun/shade	20-25cm (8-10in)	Spring
Omphalodes cappadocica, O. verna	Carpeting plants; well-drained soil, shade/sun	10-23cm (4-9in)	Late winter-summer
Polemonium caeruleum	Ferny foliage; any soil, sun/light shade	60cm (2ft)	Late spring-summer
Pulsatilla vulgaris	Downy buds, fern-like leaves, silky seed heads; rich, well-drained soil, sun	20-30cm (8-12in)	Spring
Puschkinia scilloides	Bulbous, strap-shaped leaves; rich soil, sun	10-15cm (4-6in)	Spring
Salvia haematodes, S. x superba	Bushy and branching, aromatic leaves; any soil, sun	90cm (3ft)	Summer, autumn
Sisyrinchium angustifolium, S. bermudiana, S. douglasii	Elegant narrow foliage; well-drained acid soil, sun	25-30cm (10-12in)	Early spring-summer
Stokesia laevis	Easy, long-flowering; light soil, sun/light shade	30-45cm (1-1½ft)	Summer-autumn
Thalictrum delavayi	Handsome foliage, fluffy flower clusters; any moist soil, sun/light shade	60cm (2ft)	Spring-late summer
Tradescantia x andersoniana	Strap-shaped leaves, three-petalled flowers; any moist soil, sun/light shade	45-90cm (1½-3ft)	Summer-autumn
Veronica sp. and vars.	Upright or mat-forming, attractive foliage; any well-drained soil, sun/light shade	7.5cm-1.5m (3in-5ft)	Spring-autumn

A riot of colour

The most successful border plantings are a series of informal 'pictures', an idea modelled on the long herbaceous borders of stately homes, and easily adapted to the smallest garden. The well-planned border also draws the eye throughout the year so that the fading blooms and drooping foliage of spring bulbs and early flowerers like doronicums and lupins are camouflaged by the developing stems of mid and late-season subjects.

Each 'picture' in the border needs to be composed in terms of colour associations as well as plant size and spread. As a gardener, you can concentrate on one or two dominant colours. Or you can give nature a free hand and create a border which glows exuberantly in every shade the rainbow offers. But beware: even the apparently artless arrangement of the traditional cottage garden reveals, on closer examination, the hand of the careful planner. Thus, upright groups ascend from sprawling drifts; graceful foliage plants back bold statements of colour, and the vista sweeps from neat front edgings to backdrops of tumbling climbers or compact wall shrubs.

Gaps can be filled with bright annuals, with pots of lilies sunk just below ground level, and with container-grown perennials and low shrubs. Bedding plants bring instant colour and many annuals, such as marigolds, ageratums, begonias and busy Lizzies, remain in flower until the winter.

Summer borders A kaleidoscope of colour is tempered with variegated foliage plants.

MASSED BORDER COLOUR

Create colourful borders from spring to autumn with old-fashioned favourites in close companionship.

The gardens of yesteryear were filled with the rich colours and scents of lilac and honeysuckle, jasmine and rosemary. Lavender and box surrounded wide borders brimming with colour; there was little evidence of deliberate design or colour coordination, but a passion for packing every inch of soil with brilliant flowers.

To achieve a similar effect, choose those old-fashioned plants that have retained their appeal over the years because of the rich beauty of their flowers. For early colour, try edging the border densely with crocus, hyacinths, muscaris or bellis. Follow on with the spotted foliage of lungwort,

with polyanthus in rainbow colours, the all-year rosettes of London pride, low, silver-grey mounds of old-fashioned pinks, or the endless blooms of blue catmint.

Fill the centre of the border with clumps of bright colours. For spring, choose hellebores, lupins, doronicums, irises and sweet Williams. For summer brightness choose the old favourites: sweet-scented, old shrub roses, peonies, poppies and aquilegias, valerians and campanulas, yarrows and monarda, penstemons and phlox. In autumn, there could be clumps of pink and white *Anemone × hybrida*, or dahlias, chrysanthemums and Amaryllis belladonna.

At the back of the border, climbers such as flowering ribes, forsythia, golden hop and climbing roses could be fronted with stately delphiniums, half-wild verbascums, hollyhocks, foxgloves and monkshoods.

Fill gaps with bright annuals such as marigolds, self-seeding Californian poppies, fragrant night-stock and the blue-flowered *Salvia hormium*.

▼ **Mixed borders** Shrub roses, new and old and in a variety of colours, are essential in the summer border. Tall types belong at the back, in the company of tall-stemmed blue and rosy-pink delphiniums.

▲ **Summer riot** A brick path winds towards a deliciously scented honeysuckle (*Lonicera periclymenum* 'Belgica') and a clematis, past an idyllic summer scene. Scarlet blooms of the tall *Papaver orientale* glow above white *Hesperis matronalis* 'Alba', clumps of deep blue *Iris sibirica* and, at the front, sprawling rose-pink *Centaurea dealbata*.

▶ **Gap fillers** Annual love-in-a-mist (*Nigella damascena*) is ideal for filling odd spaces in the border. Its pastel blue flowers, set among pale green, feathery foliage, bloom for many sunny weeks and are followed by handsome brown seed capsules. Black-blotched poppies (*Papaver rhoeas* 'Ladybird') make fiercely crimson statements among the blue.

▼ **Tall and stately** A narrow border is made to seem wider with a clever backdrop of old-fashioned hollyhocks (*Althaea*). The sturdy flower-studded stems tower above a veil of seeding branches from the giant sea-kale (*Crambe cordifolia*) and a front edging of white musk mallows (*Malva moschata* 'Alba').

◄ Symphony in red
Carmine spikes of Russell lupins almost match a porcelain-pink climbing rose while contrasting in colour and form with the lushly rounded blooms of double-flowered peonies. Crimson sweet Williams (*Dianthus barbatus*) add yet another shade of red at the front, relieved by a group of deep blue *Campanula glomerata*.

▼ Border profusion
Perfect, lilac-pink globes of the 1.2m (4ft) tall *Allium giganteum* jostle for attention with white Shasta daisies (*Chrysanthemum maximum*) and double-flowered salmon-orange poppies (*Papaver orientale*), which nestle close to the yellow and orange pea flowers of shrubby *Anthyllis hermanniae*. The yellow buttercups in the foreground are all but lost to the eye in this busy, early-summer scene.

OLD FASHIONED MIXTURES

You can recreate a golden age by mixing easy-to-grow low-maintenance favourites in a living tapestry of complementary colour.

You don't have to live in a rural idyll to practice the style of gardening that is traditionally associated with homes in the country. It's all a question of planning.

Plants in the traditional country-garden style conform to carefully chosen colour schemes that merge artlessly to produce a harmonious overall effect, with strategically sited foliage plants to highlight flower colours and to maintain interest when the blooms have faded. Some plants are best enjoyed in groups, others are best displayed in greater isolation.

The one significant factor in this type of gardening is the choice of plant. Pick low-maintenance plants that will look after themselves – crowding will make it difficult to reach some. Self-seeding annuals and biennials reduce yearly planting chores while clump-forming perennials will pack informal schemes. Make sure they don't need staking, pruning or much routine care.

For spring, choose bulbs that can be left in the ground, like snowdrops, crown imperial and snake's-head fritillary, scillas, daffodils and cottage tulips, and biennials and perennials that go with them – wallflowers, forget-me-nots, arabis, aubrieta and primroses, for instance.

Among the climbers which combine informal effect with minimal maintenance are honeysuckle and everlasting peas (*Lathyrus latifolius*), Virginia creeper (*Parthenocissus*), and the annual canary creeper (*Tropaeolum peregrinum*).

There are the favourite biennials, like foxgloves, sweet Williams and Canterbury bells to pack among the perennials. Just as accommodating are several annuals: cornflowers, Shirley poppies, love-in-a-mist, sunflowers.

The permanent planting can consist of lupins, flat-topped achilleas, scabious, campanulas, columbines and erigerons. For later colour use Michaelmas daisies, rudbeckias and heleniums.

Traditional path edgings include mossy saxifrages, London pride, old-fashioned pinks and several varieties of the double English daisy (*Bellis perennis*).

▼ Country-garden style
Seemingly haphazard, the predominant colours of red, white and blue in this herbaceous border are carefully separated by plantings of green, silvery and grey foliage plants.

▲ Flowers round the bath A focal point of red, white and blue has been created round a bird bath. The feathery silver foliage of *Pyrethrum ptarmaciflorum* sets off the white variegated, pink-flowered zonal pelargonium 'Mrs Parker' and an edging of sprawling, purple-blue *Campanula portenschlagiana*.

◄ Orderly disorder Fresh interest is brought to a faded border in autumn, with long plumes of squirrel-tail grass (*Hordeum jubatum*) and the bright orange seed capsules of Chinese lantern (*Physalis alkekengi*).

► Rustic charm Subtle colours epitomize the traditional English country garden. A white-flowered tree mallow (*Lavatera*) is underplanted with semi-wild foxgloves whose pastel colours are repeated in the pink Rugosa rose 'Fru Dagmar Hastrup', magenta-pink *Geranium psilostemon* and *Geranium* 'Johnson's Blue'.

◄ **Blazing red** The majestic and fragrant *Lilium speciosum* 'Rubrum' blooms in late summer, its large trumpets acknowledging the exuberant display of annual nicotianas in a full range of colours. Both species are half-hardy, and large and small trumpets will cease to blare with the first hint of autumn frost.

▼ **Colour succession** A glorious but fleeting partnership of pink oriental poppies and stately lupins is destined to be obscured by a front planting of penstemons and *Centaurea dealbata* just coming into bud. Later still, emphasis will shift to the silvery plumes of the graceful feather grass (*Stipa gigantea*) on the left.

▲ Harlequin and columbine Old favourites, the long-spurred columbines (*Aquilegia vulgaris*) come in single and checkered shades of white, pink, blue and mauve; they cross-pollinate freely and new colour variations appear from year to year. Their unusual companion is the double-flowered *Papaver* 'Fireball', a hardy perennial of uncertain parentage but with eye-catching charm.

◄ Summer freshness Like a pool of calm among the strong colours of high summer, the pure white sprays of 'Iceberg' roses rise above a sea of pale blue love-in-a-mist (*Nigella damascena*). At their feet trail and sprawl the downy, silver-grey stems and leaves of the annual *Helichrysum petiolatum*.

SUMMER BEDDING

With hundreds of dazzling bedding plants on offer from garden centres and in seed catalogues, there's a wealth of choice for attractive combinations.

Summer borders and bedding schemes are often planned mainly for vibrant colour combinations – massed reds, oranges, pinks and blues, for instance – and are most effective, but there's also scope for subtle colours and for partnerships of texture and foliage.

Summer bedding annuals make the biggest splash of colour, though many half-hardy perennials and shrubs are also treated as bedding plants for summer colour – for example wax begonias, coleus, pelargoniums and fuchsias.

Bright colour displays are very cheerful, but it's better to avoid clashes of tone and blandness of form. Those which produce an incessant blaze of colour – French marigolds (*Tagetes patula*), for in-

stance – cry out for more subtle partners when planted *en masse*.

Several annuals provide colourful yet delicate foliage, as well as floral display. Nasturtium 'Alaska' has marbled leaves and bright orange-salmon flowers, while some wax begonias have bronze foliage below red or pink flowers. Others are grown entirely for their foliage – the castor-oil plant (*Ricinus communis*) has great architectural appeal with beautiful leaves, but fairly insignificant flowers. Such plants are very effective among flowering ones, offsetting their intense colours and providing textural qualities. Filigree-fine foliage looks good against broad leaves or large flowers such as begonias.

▲ **Scarlet ladies** Flamboyant *Salvia splendens* partnered with startling red coleus and bronze marigolds do not mean to be ignored.

▼ **Floral carpet** Marigolds, begonias, pelargoniums and salvias flower all summer with vivid colours.

◄ **Silver effects** Soft and gentle contrasts are needed among the vivid colours of most bedding plants. Delicately mauve ageratums (*Ageratum houstonianum*) look stunning against the frosty, deeply cut foliage of silver-leaved cineraria (*Senecio cineraria*).

▼ **Summer meadow** Bedding schemes need not be formal or set in rigid lines and rows. Here, scattered groups of single and pompon dahlias and blue and mauve ageratums tumble among the purple spikes of *Salvia farinacea* in a tapestry of colour.

INDEX

Plants are listed under both the common name and the botanical name (which appears in italics). However, where both names are almost identical, page numbers follow the botanical name only.

ACKNOWLEDGEMENTS

Photographer's credits

Richard Balfour 123; Gillian Beckett 24(br); Biofotos/Heather Angel 21, 82, 101(b); Linda Burgess 110(b), 136; Ed Buziak 44-45; back cover; Eric Crichton 4-5, 6, 7, 8, 12(br), 17, 23(b), 24(t), 36(tr), 40, 46(tl), 46-47(b), 47(b), 48(tl,b), 55(tl,r), 61, 65, 70(tl), 72(t), 73(b), 74(b), 78, 81(tr,b), 93, 98(b), 102(br,bl), 112(b), 114(b), 122(l), 124(t,b), 126(tl), 128(b), 130(t), 137(b), 140(t,b), 142(tl), 144(t), 145, 148(tr), 150(t), 158(b), 162, 164-165(b), (Eaglemoss) 28(b), 30(t), 32(b), 114(t); Arnaud Descat 89, 112(t), 125, 155(t); Philippe Ferret 13(b), 68(b), 84, 85, 119, 156(b), 168(bl); Garden Picture Library (Brian Carter) 36(b), 37(b), 38(b), 46-47(tr), 52, 66(t), 96(t), 102(tr), 116, 142(tr), 147(tl), 150, 151, (John Glover) 45(tr), 47(tr), (Marijke Heuff) 142(b), (Anne Kelley) 166(t), (Anthony Paul) 152, (Jerry Pavia) 144(b), (Joanne Pavia) 96(b), 111, (Perdereau/Thomas) 9, 11(b), 70(bl), 71(b), 84(t), 155(b), 163, (David Russell) 23(t), (R Sutherland) 54(tl), 56(b), 148(b), (Brigitte Thomas) 64(b),

71(b), 148(b), (Didier Willery) 36(tl), (Steven Wooster) 113; John Glover 12(t), 19(bl,br), 20(b), 83, 101(t), 157(b); Derek Gould 34(b); Jerry Harpur 79, 81(tl), 109(t), 122(r), 166(b), (Abbots Ripton Hall, Cambs) 74(tr), (Eaglemoss) 172(t), (Chris Grey Wilson) 164-165(t), (Simon Hornby) 109(b), (Tintinhull House) 121, (John Vellum) 27; Marijke Heuff 57, 58, (Brummel Kemp) 167; Neil Holmes 24(bl), 70-71, Insight/Linda Burgess 72(b), 100(t); Lamontagne 90, 91, 107, 108, 117, 118, 150(b), 171; Andrew Lawson 16(t), 53, 54(tr), 56(t), 94, 95(t), 98-99; S & O Mathews 14-15, 16(b), 86(t), 126(b), 134, 146(b); Tania Midgley 39, 40-41, 41(tr), 54(tr), 99(b), 170; Natural Image (Bob Gibbons) 48(tr), 66(b), 67, (Liz Gibbons) 146(t); Philippe Perdereau 26, 31, 32-33, 42, 55(b), 59, 92(r), 110(t), 115, 120(l), 137(t), 138(b), (Brigitte Thomas) 2-3, 10, 15(b), 69, 95(b), 97; Clay Perry 138(t); Photos Horticultural 18(t), 22, 35, 38(t), 44(t), 71(tr), 86(bl), 87, 88, 127(b); Harry Smith Collection 37(t), 43, 86(tl), 128(tr), 129(t,b), 156(t); Jean-Pierre Soulier 60, 62, 92(l), 126(tr), 153, 154(b), 172(b); EWA 106, 120(r), (Karl Dietrich

Bukler) 141, (Jerry Harpur) front cover, 64(t), 73(t), 98(tl), 148(tl), 168-169(b), 169(br), Peter Woloszynski 168-169(b).

Illustrators

Ali Christie 1; Reader's Digest 20(t), 28(t), 29(tr,br), 30(b), 62, 66, 68, 84, 85, 94, 99, 100, 118, 121, 122, 135, 136(b), 138, (Dick Benson) 157, (Leonara Box) 19(t), 58, 60, 63, 80, 90, 108, 130(b), 138, (Patricia Calderhead) 82, 114, (Lynn Chadwick) 136(t), (Sara Fox Davies) 39, 41(tl), 59, 87, 89, (Brian Delf) 33(b), (Colin Emberson) 96, 102(tl), (Shirley Fells) 18(b), 88, 127, (Delyth Jones) 33(t), 44(b), 120, 165, (Nikki Kemball) 95, 146, (Josephine Martin) 107, 117, (Helen Senior) 91, (Sally Smith) 128, (Sue Stitt) 13(t), 65, 92, 115, 143, (Gill Tomblin) 12(bl), 14(b), 34(t), 42, 119, 158, 168, 170, (Barbara Walker) 11(t), 15(t), 109, 154(tr), (Ann Winterbotham) 141, 171.

Index compiled by Kate Chapman.

Typesetting SX COMPOSING, ESSEX; Printing & Binding PRINTER INDUSTRIA, GRÁFICA S.A. BARCELONA
Separations COLOURSCAN OVERSEAS CO PTE LTD, SINGAPORE

53-001-2